SEVEN DAYS TO
ONLINE
NETWORKING

*make connections to advance your
career and business quickly*

ELLEN SAUTTER
and DIANE CROMPTON

jist Works
America's Career Publisher

SEVEN DAYS TO ONLINE NETWORKING

© 2008 by Ellen Sautter and Diane Crompton

Published by JIST Works, an imprint of JIST Publishing
7321 Shadeland Station, Suite 200
Indianapolis, IN 46256-3923
Phone: 800-648-JIST   Fax: 877-454-7839   E-mail: info@jist.com

Visit our Web site at **www.jist.com** for information on JIST, free job search tips, tables of contents and sample pages, and ordering instructions for our many products!

Quantity discounts are available for JIST books. Have future editions of JIST books automatically delivered to you on publication through our convenient standing order program. Please call our Sales Department at 800-648-5478 for a free catalog and more information.

Trade Product Manager: Lori Cates Hand
Development Editor: Michelle Tullier
Copy Editor: Chuck Hutchinson
Interior Designer: Aleata Howard
Page Layout: Toi Davis
Cover Designer: Katy Bodenmiller
Proofreaders: Linda Seifert, Jeanne Clark
Indexer: Marilyn Augst

Printed in the United States of America
13 12 11 10 09 08   9 8 7 6 5 4 3 2 1

Library of Congress Cataloging-in-Publication Data

Sautter, Ellen, 1943-
   Seven days to online networking : make connections to advance your career and business quickly /
Ellen Sautter and Diane Crompton.
      p. cm.
   Includes index.
   ISBN 978-1-59357-550-2 (alk. paper)
   1. Business enterprises--Computer network resources. 2. Job hunting--Computer network resources.
3. Information resources management--Economic aspects. 4. Internet. I. Crompton, Diane, 1956-
II. Title.
   HF54.56.S28 2008
   650.1'302854678--dc22
                                    2008010828

ISBN 978-1-59357-550-2

About This Book

So you want to position yourself to land a new job or more customers for your business and know that there must be a strategic way to use the Internet to your advantage beyond just posting resumes or ads. Or perhaps you're a recruiter who needs to cast a wider net for well-qualified candidates or a salesperson who would like to find more prospects and build relationships without endless pavement-pounding. Well, online networking is what you need to be doing!

Online networking is the process of using Internet-based tools to build relationships with people for the purpose of sharing knowledge, ideas, leads, contacts, and support. The tools include social networks (a.k.a. virtual communities), blogs, discussion groups, and personal Web sites or "webfolios."

Hundreds of millions of people are networking online everyday. They're getting to know people all around the globe or in their own backyard without leaving their homes and offices. Face-to-face networking will always be important, but online networking is a convenient and powerful complement. (We tell you more about the interplay of online and offline networking in chapter 1.)

This book is designed to help you start online networking within a week, even if you're a complete beginner. Or, if you've already been dabbling in it—maybe you've set up a profile on LinkedIn and accepted a few invitations, or perhaps you've been reading and commenting on some blogs occasionally—you will now be able to take your online networking to the next level.

This hands-on, practical guide takes you from understanding what online networking is and why you should be doing it, to preparing to work the virtual room, to getting in there and actually doing it. You'll find all the information you need to start enhancing your career or business with online networking in about a week and to keep it up well beyond that time.

We've coached thousands of clients on the best ways to network online, so think of this book as our way to be by your side as you go through the process of meeting your career and business goals by connecting with the virtual world. So let's get to work together!

—Ellen Sautter and Diane Crompton

Acknowledgments

We have many people to thank for their support and assistance in the development of this book.

Our colleague and editorial consultant Michelle Tullier, a published author many times over, encouraged us to write this book and skillfully guided and supported us through the process. Lori Cates Hand, our editor at JIST, epitomizes patience, enthusiasm, and collaboration. We thank her for this opportunity.

Jim Browning, Director of Business Development for Baumgarten's, LinkedIn enthusiast, and all-around expert on social networking, generously shared his knowledge and tips. Dan Greenfield, communications executive and veteran blogger, read our manuscript and contributed valuable advice and suggestions. Walter Akana, our colleague and personal branding knowledge specialist, served as a sounding board and provided insight and inspiration. Louise Fletcher, owner of Blue Sky Resumes, as well as personal branding expert and author Kirsten Dixson, shared their expertise through informative webinars on blogging that enhanced our knowledge.

We also wish to express appreciation to our global community of colleagues at Right Management, whose enthusiasm for this project and pioneering work in online networking were such a positive influence on this book. In particular, our "family" in the Atlanta office has been a pillar of strength and support, and Davina Mazaroli was especially instrumental in contributing to the book's content.

We also thank our clients at Right, from whom we learn so much, as well as the hundreds of recruiters, job seekers, business owners, and others in our online networks who shared experiences, responded to our surveys, and asked us questions that further stimulated our research. We owe our appreciation as well to the many networking groups and industry associations that have invited us to present on this topic, giving us access to hundreds of individuals who shared their experiences with us.

Finally, we thank our family and friends, who encouraged us, read drafts, and endured many conversations on our topic. Carol Sautter was particularly helpful with research contributions and willingness to pitch in wherever needed.

Contents

A Brief Introduction to Using This Book

Networking online is a great time-saver, but it can also be a huge time-eater. With nearly 113 million blogs, millions of members on social networking sites, and literally billions of posts to message boards and discussion groups, you could easily spend every waking moment connecting with people online and still only scratch the surface. This book is organized in a way that will help you cut through the online clutter to focus on the online networking avenues that are the best use of your time.

Getting Up to Speed Within a Week

You may choose to read a chapter a day for seven days or skim through the whole book quickly in one afternoon. That's your choice. Whichever pace you choose, keep in mind that this isn't just a book to read: It's a book to work. You'll find exercises to complete, steps to follow, and online resources to check out. Don't have time for that, you say? We understand. That's why we've made it all quick and painless. All you have to do is set aside a little bit of time now to save a lot of time down the road.

If you choose to read the whole book in a day, you'll need to spend the other six days working the book—putting pen to paper or hands to keyboard to start your online networking. Or you can both read and do a chapter each day and still be done in seven days.

Where to Find the Information You Need

In chapter 1, you'll learn more about what online networking is and why it's going to benefit your job search, career, or business. In chapter 2, we help you get your ducks in a row with some important preparatory steps to take (don't even think about skipping those!). In chapter 3, we survey the seven main ways you can network online and help you see how each might match your goals. Then, in chapters 4, 5, and 6, we roll up our sleeves and walk you through the process of getting up and running on social networks, blogs, webfolios, and other tools.

Finally, in chapter 7, you'll find practical advice for making online networking a routine part of your life. You'll also find advice for continuing to expand and build both the quantity and quality of your network beyond the seventh day.

Why This Is a Short Book

We know your time is valuable. We also know how overwhelming it can be to navigate your way through the world of online networking. You need a quick, practical guide to help you start or to redirect your efforts if you've already been dabbling in online networking but lacking focus.

As career coaches, we draw on our own experiences with online networking as well as those of our clients to bring you simple but powerful advice you can put into action right away. We also pull from our backgrounds in recruiting, training, marketing, business development, and entrepreneurship to share tips that will benefit not just job seekers but also anyone who needs to expand a customer or client base for business success.

The scope of this book is not to cover every detail of developing a blog, designing a Web site, or using the most advanced features of LinkedIn or other business-oriented social networks. The topics in each chapter of this book could fill a lengthy book in their own rights, and we know that you probably don't have time to read seven books right now. You need to start moving with online networking as quickly as possible without sacrificing quality so that you can land a great job or advance in your career or business. In short, you need help in a hurry. We're happy to provide you with that help. Now, on to chapter 1!

Chapter 1

Online Networking: What It Is and Why You Should Be Doing It

Who would have thought that a former teacher and employment recruiter with no formal background in technology and a passion for coaching people face-to-face would become an advocate of networking on the Internet? And who would've thought that a career consultant known for her painstaking process of connecting clients one-by-one with just the right hand-picked person would amass her own network of millions of contacts using entirely electronic means? Well, if we can do it—and enjoy the process—so can you!

We wrote this book because we are believers in the amazing power of online networking for job seekers, entrepreneurs, recruiters, salespeople, and anyone looking to get ahead in a career or business. We've seen countless success stories from our clients and colleagues who have climbed aboard the online networking bandwagon, and we've benefited from it ourselves as well. We share some of these stories throughout the book.

In This Chapter

- What online networking is
- Why everyone needs to be doing it
- How online networking helps job seekers land jobs
- Why so many recruiters are doing it
- How salespeople and business owners can benefit

Don't just take our word for it. Millions of people are connecting with each other around the globe and in their own backyards as members of professionally oriented social network sites such as Ecademy, LinkedIn, Viadeo, XING, and more. A whopping 113 million blogs have people talking around the world (and the number will probably be higher by the time this book gets from our keyboards to your hands). Google has archived more than one billion posts to message boards and discussion groups. Any way you look at it, a lot of people are doing a lot of multinational mingling.

Not looking for a job or client halfway around the world? That's okay. Online networking has proven to be equally useful for connecting with people down the street and around the corner. The beauty is you don't have to pound the pavement or work the phones to get to them. Well, enough of this build-up. Let's look now at specifically what we mean by online networking and how it's going to enhance your life.

Online Networking Defined

Online networking is the process of using Web-based tools to connect with people for the purpose of reaching your career and business goals and, in turn, helping others reach their goals. Like traditional offline networking (meeting with people in person or speaking by telephone), online networking is an important part of any job search, personal career management plan, sales strategy, or marketing plan. Whether you call someone on the phone or write a comment on someone's blog, you're making a human-to-human connection. Whether you attend a business mixer in a hotel ballroom across town or participate in a Web-based discussion group from your home office in the basement, you're networking. It's essentially all the same thing.

The Strategy That Never Sleeps

One big difference between online networking and traditional networking, however, is that online networking is a tool that works for you 24 hours a day, 365 days a year, whether you're awake or asleep, whether you're making an effort or not. Another difference is that it gives you a reach like you've never had before. In a very short period of time—even a week—you can dramatically enlarge the scope, depth, and quality of your network in ways that traditional networking would take months, if not years, to achieve.

> ### Our Definition of Online Networking
> Online networking is the process of using Web-based tools to build relationships with people for the purpose of sharing knowledge, ideas, leads, contacts, and support. These tools include social networks (a.k.a. virtual communities), Web logs (blogs), discussion groups, listservs, and personal Web sites or "webfolios."

It's About Building Relationships

As with traditional networking, effective online networking is based on relationships. It's about getting to know people to exchange information and ideas, pass along leads and contacts, and support one another. The relationships might be somewhat short term to meet immediate objectives and goals, such as landing a job or finding a candidate to fill an open position, or they can develop into life-long professional friendships. Doesn't matter which it is. The key is to think in terms of mutually beneficial relationships that develop over time, not simply amassing lots of contacts in LinkedIn or posts on your blog.

Online networking, like any kind of networking, is as much about quality as it is quantity. It's not a numbers game or a flash-in-the-pan activity. You are developing a large network of people who know you—your talents, expertise, goals, and personality—and you, in turn, know theirs. In other words, there's substance to your network, not just a list of names.

> **Tip:** *Don't forget that building trust with the people you meet online can take time. As much as we tout the time-saving aspects of online networking, we also caution you not to assume that just because you find people online can you expect them to jump through hoops to help you. You have to earn their trust by easing into the relationship slowly, starting a dialogue, and showing that you're willing to give as much as you want to get.*

Do I Really Have Time to Network with Millions of People (and Should I Even Want To)?

Yes, you do. Yes, you should. With a minimal investment of upfront time to set yourself up online, and with a manageable investment of time to maintain your online presence, you can save huge amounts of time connecting with other people more efficiently. Do you have to get to know millions of people on a first-name basis? Of course not. But, if you have access to millions of people through common networks and shared online activities, are you more likely to be able to find just the one person you're targeting when a need arises? Of course, you are.

Finding the Needle in the Haystack

Consider the example of Gary P., a senior executive searching for a new job due to a restructuring at his previous company. He heard about opportunities at a global consulting firm, a logical target for his background. Unfortunately, he didn't know anyone there and neither did members of his immediate traditional network. So he approached his career coach at one of Right Management's offices in Virginia. That person e-mailed his colleagues in other Right offices to enlist their help.

Ellen, in the Atlanta office of Right, received the e-mail. Although she couldn't think of anyone she knew personally at that company off the top of her head, she checked her LinkedIn network and instantly identified 126 people currently with that firm! These were people who knew people that she knew.

The contacts were located in 11 different U.S. cities and in 10 other countries on three continents. Gary wanted high-level contacts in the organization, and the 126 people included 8 Associate Directors, 3 Principals, 4 Directors, 18 Vice Presidents, 13 Managing Directors, a Human Resources Manager, the Chief Technology Officer, and the Co-founder and Owner! Gary was able to select the contacts he deemed most appropriate based on their levels, locations, and LinkedIn profiles and get introduced to them through the LinkedIn network!

With online networking, you experience greatly enhanced efficiencies in your self-marketing or business development efforts. You reach more people more quickly—and not just more people, but the right people. Online networking is a networking accelerator that puts you on the fast track toward your goals. Imagine how long it would have taken Gary or his consultant in the "Finding the Needle in the Haystack" example to find the contacts he needed at his target company. They would have had to search databases or directories to find the names of people who work for that company and then call or send e-mail to hundreds of people to hit upon someone who knew any of the names they'd targeted. This could have taken days or weeks unless they happened to get lucky and make a connection more quickly.

The Luck of LinkedIn

With online networking, you don't have to rely on luck. You rely on the six degrees of separation idea, although with sites such as LinkedIn, it's really more about two to three degrees of separation. All it took was the consultant in Virginia e-mailing other consultants to request the inside track to this particular company. All Ellen had to do was spend a few seconds doing a keyword search in her LinkedIn network to come up with 126 names of people at that company who know people that she knows.

Much More Than Your 15 Minutes of Fame

Online networking also saves time and opens you up to a wider array of career or business opportunities because it lets you network passively. You are more visible to the world, and the world is more visible to you. Since you haven't been living under a rock for the past several years, you already know that a business with a Web site reaches a much broader audience of potential customers than one that has to rely on putting up signs in the neighborhood or mailing out brochures and flyers (paid attention to much junk mail lately?). The Web site serves as an online brochure that advertises the business 24/7 and that isn't tossed into the trash can with the junk mail.

> **Tip:** Wondering just how visible you really are? You probably already know that Web sites and blogs can have a built-in ticker that counts the number of visitors, but did you know there are also ways to track your visibility even if you don't want to have your own site or blog? Sites such as Naymz.com and Ziggs.com let you post a profile to establish your online identity and then notify you by e-mail each time your profile is viewed.

Whether you have a business to advertise or simply want to be visible as an individual to attract opportunities, you can do so with your own webfolio, blog, or online profile posted on a networking site. You can also do so by participating in online discussion groups and other people's blogs. When you take 15 minutes to post your thought for the day—not your thoughts on what you had for breakfast but some relevant piece of information for people in your field—you reap the benefits of hours and hours and hours of people getting to know you by reading that post in the days or weeks that follow. Or, if you've written a whole article for a Web site or a short comment on a blog that has staying power, your archived information might be read for months and years to come.

Everybody Wins

In later sections of this chapter, we cover the benefits that specific groups of people may enjoy through online networking. Job seekers, the self-employed, employment recruiters, salespeople, and any career-oriented individual looking to be more successful will find specific reasons for networking online. But some reasons to do it are benefits common to everyone. Let's take a look at those:

- **It's 24/7 networking.** Your profile and other content that you create online work for you day and night. The Internet never closes!

- **It's a screening tool.** You can get to know a lot about a person through his or her online identity before investing the time in building a relationship. By reading someone's profile or webfolio or by viewing the quality of that person's contributions to blogs or discussion groups, you evaluate whether someone's knowledge, experience, and style are compatible with the goals you have for your network.

- **It gives unprecedented access with the utmost convenience.** You can participate in multiple networking "meetings" in the same day or evening from your computer, putting you in touch with hundreds or thousands of people you would not otherwise have been able to meet, or at least could not have met so quickly.

- **It's less threatening and intimidating.** Many people, especially introverts, find face-to-face or phone networking challenging. Networking from the comfort of your own computer screen can be much less intimidating. Online networking isn't a substitute for picking up the phone or showing up at a networking event, but it can be a less scary way to meet people and start to build professional relationships that can then be moved offline.

- **It lets you show off your technical skills and appear tech savvy.** Online networking requires such basic technical skills that even a computer novice or technophobe can do it successfully and appear in-the-know.

- **It gives you a wide platform for communicating who you are.** Your talents, expertise, and unique selling points—all the things that make up "brand you"—can be conveyed to a broad yet targeted audience.

- **It's a way to build your credibility.** All online networking venues offer an opportunity to share your knowledge with others, whether through blogging, Question & Answer areas of social networks, or participation in discussion groups.

- **It levels the playing field.** If you have a physical disability, or if your outward appearance or speaking voice is not your best asset, networking from behind a computer screen is ideal. You can build relationships without other people's personal biases getting in the way. And, if you have mobility issues, you can enjoy connecting with people from the convenience of home.

- **It's a springboard to offline meetings, appointments, and relationships.** Online networking is not a substitute for traditional face-to-face networking; it's a catalyst for those relationships.

Clearly, the benefits are many and the downsides are few. What is the downside to online networking? For starters, you have to watch how you spend your time. If you're already someone who spends time browsing or researching on the Internet, you know how the time can fly by before you realize it. Online networking is the same. You could spend all day blogging, tweaking the content on your webfolio, and poking around in social networks to see who's who. Online networking can be a major time-eater, so you have to set limits on how much time you spend doing it on a daily or weekly basis.

> **Tip:** Worried about privacy, personal security, and spam issues that might arise from making yourself so visible in cyberspace? Although it's prudent to have some concern and be careful, most online networking venues allow you to control how people get your contact information. You can choose the level of anonymity you want.

You also have to be careful not to focus all your energy on online networking and not spend enough time connecting with people offline. Online networking is not a substitute for getting out of the house or office and attending networking events, meeting people for lunch or coffee, or picking up the phone to have a live conversation.

Why Job Seekers Must Get Online (and We Don't Just Mean Posting Your Resume on Monster!)

Deborah G., a marketing communications manager, found the ideal position on a major job board and submitted her resume online. Not content with simply firing off her resume into cyberspace and sitting back to wait for a reply that might never come, she set out to find a contact inside the company. Problem was, she didn't know anyone at that organization. And as a relatively new member of LinkedIn with a small network on that site, her search of her LinkedIn network also yielded no connections.

Fortunately, Deborah knew someone with a large LinkedIn network. That person found 32 contacts at the company. In reviewing the list, Deborah was surprised and pleased to discover the name of a former colleague who had gone on to work for the company where she had just applied. She e-mailed him and found him happy to hear from her and glad to help out. He presented Deborah to the hiring manager and also coached her on interviewing strategy given his knowledge of the organization. She landed the job!

Ray L., an IT executive, decided to start a blog to showcase his skills and build a personal brand for his executive-level job search. Within two months of launching his blog, he counted over 1,300 views of his online bio and resume. Eight opportunities had been presented and had yielded four interviews. And he had scheduled five speaking engagements! Clearly, the blog was an effective marketing vehicle for his job search.

The Answer to Your Job Search Dilemma

As career consultants, we coach job seekers everyday, and we see what works and what doesn't in a job search. We work for a global career transition firm in the field commonly known as "outplacement." Outplacement firms provide services to people who are terminated from their jobs, most often through no fault of their own. When organizations downsize due to mergers, acquisitions, restructuring, or other factors, they provide our firm's career transition services to the departing employees. We don't place people in jobs like recruiters do; we coach them through the process to be the best possible job candidates they can be.

We see job seekers who haven't been on the market in decades as well as those who have changed jobs every couple of years. We work with clients who barely have the technical skills to send an e-mail and others who are IT specialists. Some have job skills that are in high demand, whereas others have to work hard to update their skills and appear employable. We assist candidates at all levels, in a wide variety of industries and functional areas. Job hunts come in all shapes and sizes, but one characteristic is constant: A job search is most likely to come to a successful conclusion, and a quicker one, when the job seeker networks actively.

Landing jobs through online job boards such as Monster, CareerBuilder, and the many other employment sites out there is gaining momentum, especially for those with clearly defined, tangible skills such as IT or accounting professionals. But word-of-mouth—or networking—is still the way most job seekers find their next position. The word-of-mouth method has typically consisted of calling, e-mailing, and meeting with people you know, or people they know, to let them know you're looking, as well as attending networking events to meet new people. This form of networking will always be a critical element of a job search. There's no substitute for traditional, offline networking as the best way to build meaningful professional relationships. But now, with online networking, you can propel your networking efforts into a whole new dimension.

How Online Networking Fits into a Job Search

Don't misunderstand us; we don't mean that if you join LinkedIn or set up a blog, the job offers will start pouring in. (Well, they actually might, but we're not making any promises!) Just as with traditional networking, you have to be strategic about how you use online networking to get to a job offer, or even just to find the opportunities and reach the interview stage. Next, we describe some of the ways you might use online networking in your job search.

Get Information and Advice

As you attempt to define your career goals and job objectives, you can find people online who might help with your decision-making and focusing process. This is particularly important if you are considering changing career fields—your functional role or industry—but also helpful for staying up on trends and developments in your existing field to help identify new areas of opportunity.

Identify Potential Employers to Target

After you define an employment objective, you need to come up with a "hit list" of employers that you'd like to work for based on the criteria you've identified as important to you. Databases, directories, chamber of commerce listings, and magazines and journals for your field are all tried-and-true methods for finding organizations you might want to work for, but now online networking adds another source. You can search the memberships of social networks to see where people work, can read company blogs to get a feel for various corporate cultures, and can ask people in your online networks which organizations they recommend for your list.

Find Specific People Within Your Targeted Organizations

When you have your "hit list" developed, your next step is to approach someone within the organization by phone or e-mail to let that person know about your interest in working there or to request an informational interview to explore the possible fit between your skills and the organization's needs. You need to identify the right person to connect with and not just send a "To Whom It May Concern" type of inquiry to the human resources department. You might also see job listings online or in other sources and want to find someone specific to talk to instead of applying somewhat anonymously. Just as you saw in our earlier example of Deborah G., you can leverage your membership in virtual communities to find the best person to talk with.

Be More Visible to Recruiters and Employers

Executive search consultants, recruiters in staffing agencies, and internal recruiters in companies are flocking to the Internet in droves to find candidates to fill positions. By having a well-written profile on LinkedIn or other virtual communities, by having a webfolio to serve as an online resume of sorts, and by being active on blogs to show off your knowledge, you will attract recruiters and hiring managers.

Feel Supported Through the Ups and Downs

A job search can be a long, arduous process. As part of online communities, you can receive valuable advice, support, and encouragement to help you through the rough patches.

With the average tenure on a job in the United States currently at about four years, establishing the long-term relationships that are critical to developing a solid network is becoming more and more difficult. When you need to look for a job, you might find that you and all your colleagues have moved around so much that you don't have much of a grounded network. By incorporating online networking techniques, you can greatly enhance the size and quality of your network and make your job search go much more smoothly.

> **Tip:** Remember that everything you say and do online leaves a digital trail that reflects either positively or negatively on your reputation and character. It's natural for job seekers to want to vent their frustrations, but be careful what, where, and to whom you do that online. You don't want prospective employers to see you as a whiner!

Why Recruiters Should Use Online Networking Tools

The recruiting business has always been and will always be a people business. Recruiters, for the most part, are effective networkers offline. But technology and the Internet have certainly changed the way that recruiters do business or should be doing business, and online networking is a big part of those changes.

Although some recruiters might be into blogging or participating in online discussion groups, we especially see recruiters using the social networking sites. As the largest of the social networking sites, LinkedIn is a favorite tool of recruiters. According to a popular blog about LinkedIn, more than 200,000 recruiters are members of this site, and that number is growing every day. Many recruiters have very large networks on LinkedIn, indicating that they see great value in this form of online networking and have chosen to invest time in building and maintaining their networks.

We conducted some informal surveys of recruiters to ask about their usage of and reactions to LinkedIn. We heard the following:

- LinkedIn is a great professional tool.

- Candidates should use LinkedIn extensively. They should be using LinkedIn *before* they are out of a job!

- LinkedIn is a great tool for business development, candidate sourcing, and job posting.

- We use LinkedIn to find people with specific qualifications and experience, and it works really well.

- Two years ago, we were using four major job boards to find candidates. We've now dropped three job boards and purchased the corporate solution from LinkedIn.

These comments were representative of the larger pool of survey responses. No respondent expressed negative comments about LinkedIn, and all suggested that it is now a key part of their business process.

Post a Profile and They Will Come

Michelle A., a job seeker client at Right Management, was recently hired by a recruiting firm for an administrative role. The firm found her on LinkedIn, indicating that recruiters are using it to fill positions internally as well as to find candidates for their client companies. She happily accepted the recruiting firm's offer but was delighted to report that three other prospective employers had also contacted her based on her LinkedIn profile! She's a LinkedIn member for life!

So how do recruiters benefit from networking online? Online networking assists recruiters with every aspect of their business—including sourcing candidates, marketing their services to companies, and forming partnerships with other recruiters.

Finding Candidates

LinkedIn and other social networking sites provide recruiters with exactly the information they need—data on millions of candidates in diverse industries, with a broad range of functional skills and levels of experience, and in every location imaginable. It's all there and easily accessible thanks to some pretty effective search engines.

Other factors further enhance the benefits:

- **Accurate information:** The information tends to be more accurate and more current than information found in databases and directories because individuals provide the information themselves and can update it easily and immediately as things change.

- **Access to passive candidates:** Unlike the job boards, which primarily feature information about active job seekers, LinkedIn and other social networking sites include what recruiters call "passive" job seekers—people who aren't in an active job search but who might be receptive to a new opportunity. Although recruiters in today's layoff-prone society are less reluctant to present unemployed candidates to their clients than in earlier decades, still, presenting candidates who are not already "in the market" is often their preference and makes it easier to justify their fees.

- **Access to hard-to-find candidates:** LinkedIn and other sites help recruiters find people deep down in a company, people who previously weren't easily located. In pre-online networking eras, it was always a challenge to identify a design engineer or programmer or people in other nonleadership roles who weren't listed in business directories. Now, those folks are visible and accessible on LinkedIn.

- **Candidate evaluation:** Viewing self-submitted candidate information gives recruiters a chance to see how candidates present themselves online, in particular their written communication skills and attention to detail.

- **Reference checking capability:** Through the social networking sites, recruiters can do "unofficial" background checks. On LinkedIn, recruiters can view "endorsements" or references that bosses, colleagues, subordinates, vendors, and customers can post for an individual. But beyond that, recruiters can identify and approach individuals not on an official reference list to hear about their candidates. Or they can do a search on Google or another search engine to check out a candidate's electronic footprint.

In addition to searching for just the right candidate, recruiters can also post jobs on LinkedIn and other social networking sites to draw a broad candidate response, possibly from people who didn't have a profile on the site. (You can see jobs posted on LinkedIn whether or not you have a profile on the site.)

And candidate sourcing is also about networking. Maybe that perfect candidate isn't profiled on the social networking site. But chances are, someone on the site knows that perfect candidate and can provide the recruiter with an introduction.

Marketing and Business Development

Recruiters need to market their services effectively to win business, and they can find prospective clients on LinkedIn and other social networking sites. Online networking strategies can greatly enhance a recruiter's business development efforts.

- **Networking opportunities:** Just as most new jobs come from networking, so do most new clients. So the enhanced networking opportunities on sites like LinkedIn can give recruiters greater access to more people and more prospects.

- **Building credibility:** LinkedIn and other comparable sites provide an opportunity to build credibility, more than just words on a Web site. Approaching a prospect through a common connection, showing that you are well networked and someone good to know, can help to gain a prospect's trust.

- **Communicating brand:** And just as job seekers need to have a complete and enticing profile on the social networking sites, recruiters need to communicate their brand and promote themselves through their profile data, data that works 24/7 to attract new business.

Identifying Recruiters for Split-Fee Collaboration

Recruiters often partner with other recruiters to make cooperative placements. Sharing job orders and resumes can add to each firm's capabilities and provide a better and faster response to a client. Some recruiters are members of recruiter networks that provide built-in processes for collaboration and information sharing. Online networking sites such as LinkedIn can provide additional resources to identify potential alliance partners and create new revenue opportunities.

Recruiter Beware

Although the use of social networking sites can have an overwhelmingly beneficial impact on the business of recruiting, it's not all positive. Two areas can create problems for recruiters.

One is the open nature of social networking sites—the model of sharing contacts without expectation of a fee—that can conflict with the fee-based nature of the recruiting business. What happens when a candidate asks a recruiter for an introduction to his or her client on LinkedIn? We can't say what happens all the time because we've seen it work both ways. One recruiter we know consistently makes the online introductions as requested. One of our job seeker clients, on the other hand, had his request for an introduction denied by the recruiter he contacted. That recruiter opted to meet with the job seeker herself to be able to represent him to her client. Her action was somewhat outside the spirit of LinkedIn, yet was understandable and may offer more support and be of greater benefit to the job seeker in the long run.

A second challenge for recruiters is that the access they have to this huge global database of active and passive candidates is not exclusive. Internal recruiters and hiring managers can access candidates there too, creating additional competition for recruiters. This isn't a new phenomenon, however. Companies have always had and frequently exercised the option of hiring directly to avoid third-party fees. Yet, experienced and effective recruiters will continue to be able to offer convincing cost-benefit justifications for their services.

Online networking, specifically the use of social networking sites including LinkedIn, offers great advantages to recruiters. Just as job seekers and business owners can network more efficiently, connect to a broader audience, tap into rich information resources, communicate their brand more easily, and create and close opportunities online, recruiters too can market their services, identify candidates, complete search assignments, and form collaborative partnerships with other recruiters...and likely do it all faster using online networking strategies.

Note: *LinkedIn has become known as a favorite site for recruiters, but it's by no means the only social networking site out there. In chapter 4, we tell you more about additional sites, such as Ecademy, XING, and more, and help you see which ones might be the best fit for you.*

How Salespeople, Entrepreneurs, and Anyone with a Business to Develop or a Product to Market Can Benefit

Cultivating business relationships face-to-face, or at least through frequent phone contact, is a critical element of business development. We don't deny that in the least. You have to get out there and call on your customers and clients as well as knock on the doors of your prospects. You also have to show up at networking meetings, conferences, and any events that are relevant to your targets; that is, go to the places where your customers congregate or where the people who could refer business to you congregate. You also have to do some wining and dining, bonding with your clients over meals, on the golf course, and at any sporting, arts, or social events that your client would enjoy being treated to. None of that has changed or is likely ever to change.

There's no substitute for face time, but what if you could use the Internet to get a foot in the door so you can get that face time? Or what if you could use it to have the inside track that gives you an edge in writing a proposal or making a sales presentation? That's what online networking can do.

If you skipped over the sections of this chapter that described online networking for job seekers, please go back and read them. Job seekers market themselves to potential employers. As a salesperson, freelancer, or business owner, you market yourself to potential customers who could use your product, service, or expertise. So the benefits of online networking for job seekers are much the same as those for salespeople and entrepreneurs. You can be more strategic in how you go after business, can be more visible so that the business comes to you, and can get ideas from others that might enhance your own success. Next, we describe the advantages.

Attracting Customers or Clients

When you are visible online, whether through membership in a social network or by blogging or having a webfolio, you don't always have to be pounding the pavement to find people to buy your product or service or to find your next gig if you're self-employed.

Generating Referrals

When you participate in blogs or discussion groups, people get to know you as a representative of your organization and will turn to you when they hear of someone who needs to do business with someone in your space. Because they see you online and read what you have to say, and because your communications there sound more genuine and less like marketing collateral or Web site content, they come to feel like they know and trust you and will feel comfortable telling other people about you.

Identifying Targets

Scouring the membership of online social networks and checking out blogs and discussion groups to see who's talking are great ways to identify people who might need to know about you and your products or services.

Selling Strategically

You do your due diligence on a prospect before you make your first call or design that first PowerPoint slide for a sales presentation. You probably ask around among people you know to see if anyone has the inside scoop on the individual or organization. You probably do some research online to see what you can find. Well, with online networking, you can be more focused in your strategizing. You can find people in your virtual communities who have the insights and inside track you need to get the competitive advantage.

Finding Money!

As an entrepreneur, you might need to secure venture-capital funds or find angel investors. Sure, traditional research methods work well, and face-to-face meetings are critical, but by also turning to virtual communities where investors might be members, you can reach your hand much deeper into the honey pot.

Using a Blog to Find New Clients

An entrepreneur that we know in the career coaching business is an avid blogger, using that low-cost vehicle combined with equally cost-effective traditional networking to market her services. In her pre-blog era, her clients came to her largely from word-of-mouth advertising. Today she attributes 90 percent of her business to the Internet and her blog. In her blog postings, she showcases her skills and services in a credible and subtle manner instead of having to resort to hard-sell strategies, thereby winning the trust and confidence of prospective clients. Not all her new clients read her blog. But some do, and others are referred by people who read her blog.

We've experienced the revenue-generating benefits of online networking ourselves. Although business development is not our primary function at Right, by networking online and being visible to decision makers at companies, we receive inquiries about our company's products and services, often from companies that our business development team has never contacted or from organizations that our sales staff had not been able to penetrate.

So what are you waiting for? Get online and start enjoying the same kinds of successes!

Why Everyone with a Career Needs to Network Online

You're reasonably happy with the job you do and the employer you work for. You stay relatively busy at work most days, maybe even extremely busy. You know that you ought to be networking to stay connected to people in your field and to have people to turn to in case you end up needing to look for a new job in the future. You try to go to your professional association or industry meetings and conferences from time to time, and you try to meet for lunch with acquaintances from other organizations, but you often feel guilty for not doing enough of this—or maybe for not doing it at all. It's just too hard to find the time and the motivation.

Well, online networking might be your answer. Instead of having to struggle to break away from work, fight traffic, and find the energy to attend an after-hours networking meeting, you can connect with people online through blogging, discussion groups, or e-mail exchanges with fellow social network members. Instead of spending hours writing articles for your field's professional journals or lining up speaking engagements to be visible in your field, you can gain even broader visibility by having your own blog or webfolio. Sure, you have to make the effort to keep your content current on the blog or Web site, but you can do that whenever and wherever it's convenient for you.

We're not saying that you shouldn't still make an effort to be visible in the traditional ways—writing or speaking in your field, or perhaps taking a leadership role in a professional association that meets face-to-face—but you can use the Internet-based methods to your advantage as well.

Whether you work in the corporate world or the nonprofit or public sectors, if someone else employs you and cuts your paycheck, you cannot afford to be complacent about your job security. You've probably figured out by now that no one is indispensable. Maybe you've been the victim of job cuts or have witnessed close friends or family members suddenly losing their jobs despite having done great work for their employers. It happens to dedicated factory workers, seemingly

> **Tip:** *Even if you're not in job search mode currently, don't hesitate to build relationships with recruiters online. You never know when you might need them in the future.*

indispensable administrative assistants, highly skilled technical workers, and the most senior executives. No one is immune. Organizational restructuring and downsizing, outsourcing and offshoring, economic and political factors, and a host of other catalysts are all constantly churning up the job market.

In our career coaching roles, hardly a day goes by that we don't hear one of our clients express regret over the fact that he or she didn't maintain an active network while still employed. "If only I had stayed in touch with people and forced myself to get out to networking events, I wouldn't feel like I'm starting my network from scratch now," they say. Perhaps if they had known how much can be done online, they would have been able to keep up their networks better. Now, you have a golden opportunity not to let yourself get in the same predicament. Some of the ways you might benefit from online networking now rather than later are outlined in the following sections.

Make Better Career Decisions

By having a huge network of professional colleagues at your fingertips, you can get valuable input on new directions you might want your career to go, whether within your current organization or elsewhere. You can check out new roles, new industries, and new markets. You can also get feedback from others on whether to accept a promotion or relocation opportunity you've been offered.

See What's Out There

As you interact with, or read the profiles of, other people online, you get a bigger-picture view of the employers and roles and professions that exist than you would if you stayed in your own bubble. You'll either find that you've got it pretty good where you are and ought to stay put, or that the grass looks greener somewhere else.

Position Yourself for Raises and Promotions

We don't claim that plum jobs and big money will come raining down on you like manna from cyberheaven just because you blog or join a social network. What we do know, however, is that the more you present yourself to the world as a well-connected mover and shaker in your field, the more your own employer will see that your professional stature is an asset to the organization. And, if your boss or boss's boss can't see that, you might need to move on! Your blog can help you do that as well.

Attract Opportunities Like a Magnet

Let's say you aren't actively looking for a new job, but you're always open to exploring opportunities that might bring you more job satisfaction or a fatter paycheck. Well, when you have a profile posted online, whether through a social network site or your own Web site, or when you share your knowledge by posting on blogs related to your profession or industry, you become what recruiters call a passive candidate. They can easily find you to tell you about jobs you didn't even know you were interested in.

Enhance and Share Your Knowledge Base

Believe it or not, successful career management is not all about you! It's not all about getting better jobs, coveted assignments, or more money. It's also about learning, growing, and giving back to others. By connecting with people online, you can share your knowledge and soak up ideas and information from others, all the while enhancing your performance and making your work life more stimulating and interesting.

If you carve out some time from your busy work schedule to get involved online in some way, you too can reap the benefits outlined in this section.

> **Tip:** *Woodrow Wilson is credited with saying "I not only use all the brains that I have, but all that I can borrow." Keep this philosophy in mind as you network. Sharing knowledge with your professional community and not trying to solve all your career or work problems yourself is wise advice.*

I Know What It Is and Why I Should Do It, So What Now?

Before diving into online networking, you'll need to take some simple preparatory steps. In chapter 2, we help you get your ducks in a row so that you can start benefiting from online networking as soon as possible. So let's get on with it!

Key Points: Chapter 1

- Online networking is the process of using Web-based tools to connect with people for the purpose of reaching your career and business goals and, in turn, helping others reach their goals.

- Even if you're not actively trying to find or fill a job or develop new business, you can enhance your professional stature, security, and performance by connecting with people online.

- Online networking is a convenient complement to traditional networking in that it gives unprecedented access to more people more easily.

- Through online networking, job seekers can get advice about their search techniques, identify employers to target, get introduced to key decision-makers, and become visible to recruiters.

- Recruiters are flocking to online networking venues in large numbers to source hard-to-find candidates, verify candidates' credentials, develop business, and form strategic alliances.

- By networking online, salespeople and entrepreneurs can identify and check out prospects, be introduced to potential customers, and find sources of funding.

Chapter 2

How to Stand Out in the Cyberspace Crowd

Now that you've learned what online networking is and why you should be doing it, you might feel ready to dive right in and start networking. Maybe you're ready to join social networks, start a blog or write a comment on one, or perhaps whip up a Web site. Because some of these things are so easy to do, we've had people create a blog or join LinkedIn in less than five minutes while sitting in the audience of our training sessions. (We thought they were hanging on our every word and taking notes on their laptops, but they were already off and running, putting our words into action!)

> ### In This Chapter
>
> - Stand out from your competition on the Internet.
> - Determine what sort of identity you have online, if any.
> - Deal with negative online information about you.
> - Develop your self-marketing sound bite—a key communication tool.

We appreciate that enthusiasm, but we recommend slowing down just a little bit. Sure, this book is all about getting up and running with online networking in seven days, so every minute counts. But we don't want you to plow ahead until you've done some critical preparation. We know it sounds boring, but it's really important, so bear with us.

Your Online Identity: What It Is and Why You Need One

Every step you take online creates your online identity. Your online identity is your professional image. It's how people see you. It's your personal brand. Just as large companies have images and reputations, known as their

brands, you have a brand as well. Your knowledge, skills, contributions, accomplishments,
goals, values, communication style, personality, and even physical appearance (if you post
photos of yourself) all make up your brand,
or online identity.

Having an online identity is becoming
increasingly important for all sorts of
professionals. In the past, a business card and
nameplate on your office door or a resume
and interview suit were all you needed to
establish yourself as "real" in the minds of
others. Of course, the quality of your work
and ethical standards were—and still are—the
essential substance behind the window dress-
ing, but your professional image and identity
were primarily conveyed through these nonelectronic outer trappings.
These days, your presence online is just as important as the old-fashioned
image-makers.

> **Tip:** Don't skip this chapter! Online net-working puts you in front of millions of people with one touch of the Enter key on your computer. Almost every piece of content you put on the Internet forges your online identity for years to come, so don't venture into online networking without first being pre-pared.

Your online identity is like a trail of footprints in the sand. Every move you
make online and even some offline moves that are chronicled online create
a trail of digital tracks in the cybersands.

If There's No Evidence of You Online, Do You Exist?

Recruiters and employers, as well as prospective clients or customers, now
expect to find you online. They turn to the Internet to scope out your credentials, opinions, and even appearance. If you have no online presence (a
search engine turns up no matches for your name), or even worse, a negative online presence (a search engine brings up unfavorable or irrelevant
information about you), you need to develop or improve your online identity to stand head and shoulders above the competition.

> *"It is now common knowledge that your name and your identity leave an
> indelible impression online, making reputation management a new-
> century skill. Anything that is connected to your name on the Internet can
> be viewed as a reflection of your character and integrity...."*
>
> —Dave Opton, CEO and Founder, ExecuNet in "Dealing with Your
> Digital Dirt 2.0," 2006 ExecuNet, Inc.

In this chapter, we introduce you to the building blocks of creating your online identity. In chapter 3, you'll continue to build your presence online with further guidance from us. Our aim is to help you stand out by being carefully, not carelessly, visible.

This is a working chapter in which you'll complete some simple exercises to start developing your online identity, so enter your thoughts directly into the worksheets provided later in this chapter or type them on your computer if you prefer.

What to Do If Too Many People with Your Name Exist Online

The opposite problem of not having enough of a presence online is having too many of you present online! If your name is fairly common, you might find that lots of other people who share your name have left a digital trail that is not yours. And sometimes it's a trail you'd rather not be associated with.

This common dilemma has various solutions. You can start to create a name for yourself—a unique name—by including an initial rather than only first and last name when you do anything in public offline or online. You can also more aggressively build up your digital presence so that the first matches for Mary Jones or John Smith are you and not someone else.

Following Your Digital Footprints

Before establishing yourself online, you need to know what's already out there about you. If prospective employers decide to look you up online, what will they find, if anything? If potential customers want to know more about you as the owner of a business they might deal with, how much will they find online about you? The first thing most people are likely to do when they want to learn more about you is to look you up using a search engine. Google is arguably the most popular search engine, so that's where we'll start.

Go Google Yourself

Your first step in assessing your online identity is to Google yourself. Simply type your name into the keyword search field of www.google.com and see what comes up. Use variations of your name, such as with or without a middle initial, or use your formal first name instead of a nickname.

Also, be sure to put quotation marks around your name so that only exact matches will come up. Otherwise, you'll end up pulling up content that includes your first and last name but not necessarily the two names together. If your name is common enough that it's likely to pull up results for many other people, try combining your name with a company you're employed by (or have been employed by in the past) or your business name. Use the plus symbol to add these additional criteria to your search. Example: "Ann Jackson" + "Western Airlines."

> **Tip:** Don't forget about other search engines! Just because Google gets all the attention doesn't mean you should ignore other search tools such as About, AlltheWeb, AltaVista, Ask, ChaCha, Dogpile, GigaBlast, MSN, and Yahoo!.

Don't drive yourself crazy feeling that you must look yourself up on every search engine all the time. You can limit your regular (weekly or monthly) monitoring to Google and one or two other sites, but keep the full list on hand so that you can check all of them periodically. To find a comprehensive list of search engines beyond those listed here, consult www.searchenginewatch.com.

How Do You Look Online?

As you browse the results of your search, ask yourself the following three questions to determine how strong and favorable your online identity is:

- **How many?** The *quantity* of results is important. The higher your stature and longer your tenure in your professional or business arena, the more hits you should have.

- **So what?** Asking yourself this question helps you determine the *relevance* of your matches. Do search engines direct people to the most relevant information about you? The Google (or other search engine) results for a search of your name should lead viewers down a digital path lined with hallmarks of your personal brand. It's okay to have some results that reflect nonprofessional areas of your life, such as community service and recreational or social activities, as long as those activities don't reflect negatively on the professional image you want to convey.

- **What good does it do?** How *positive or negative* are the results of your search? Does the search dig up information from your past that you'd rather someone not see? Or are the results positive—helping to enhance your professional stature or build credibility for your business?

By taking this first step of Googling yourself, you get a handle on what your online identity starting point is. Do you have negative information to clean up, or not enough information at all? Do you need to create more relevant, positive hits for your name? Next, we look at what you can do to establish the best possible online identity.

> **Tip:** When you Google yourself, go beyond the usual Web text search and check also for images, video, news, blogs, and other search options that might bring up matches for your name. On the Google home screen, simply click on one of those choices, usually located near the top of the screen, and then type your name in quotation marks in the search field and see what comes up.

Taking Background Checks Online

According to a 2007 survey of employment recruiters conducted by ExecuNet, 83 percent of recruiters have used search engines to uncover information about candidates, and more than 43 percent have ruled out candidates based on information found online about them. Clearly, your online identity and digital dirt play a significant role in your job search success.

Cleaning Up Your Digital Dirt

The term "digital dirt" was coined in the 2005 ExecuNet report "Dealing with Your Digital Dirt" to describe negative information lurking on the Internet that can damage reputations, cause embarrassment, prevent job seekers from getting hired, and even get people fired.

What Is Digital Dirt?

Digital dirt comes in all shapes and sizes and varying degrees of lethality. Typical examples of digital dirt are the following:

- Personal information you'd rather not share in the workplace

- Controversial associations, opinions, or memberships

- Embarrassing evidence of unprofessional behavior (such as photos of yourself appearing drunk and wild at a party)

- Public records or references to lawsuits or felonies

- Information about your credentials that contradicts data on your resume or business marketing materials and therefore reveals you to be lying

- Evidence of a moonlighting business that could be a conflict of interest with, or distraction from, your primary work

Digital dirt doesn't have to be disastrous. It can be simply something that is irrelevant to your professional reputation and distracts people from the real message you want to get across about who you are and what you have to offer. Regardless of how dirty your dirt is, it's something you'd rather not have. We'll now help you see what sort of action you can take against it.

An Example of Distracting, but Not Damaging, Digital Dirt

Consider the case of a management consultant we know. She was married in 1996 and had a wedding announcement published in the *New York Times* that year. In 2007 she Googled herself and discovered that despite 20-plus years of professional accomplishments—several published books and magazine articles, lots of public speaking, and various bios posted online—her 11-year-old wedding announcement was the first search result that came up at the top of a list of 15,600 Google hits about her! She certainly wasn't ashamed of being married, nor was it anything she wanted to keep secret, but an 11-year-old wedding announcement was not exactly the first thing she wanted people to see when going online to get to know her professionally. Why was this happening? The *New York Times* is such a powerful online media outlet that Google is likely to pull up a name that has appeared in that newspaper before other newer, but less heavily trafficked sites.

How to Clean Up Your Digital Dirt

If you have negative information or irrelevant information that bugs you, you have three choices for getting rid of it:

- **Wash over it.** Create so much new online content about yourself that the negative or irrelevant information is buried under fresher, more relevant, and more positive content. This method is also useful when you're dealing with digital content that relates to someone else who shares your name. The more positive, relevant content you can create that is truly yours, the more you'll stand out from the pack of Jane Smiths and John Does.

- **Wash it out.** Get rid of it entirely. Having online content deleted is not easy. Unless you or someone you know well created or posted the content in the first place, you might have a difficult time getting the owners of sites to remove the offending content.

- **Wait it out.** Take no active measures to hide or delete the content, but just let nature take its course. Nature, in this case, is the natural sequence of events in most reasonably active, visible professionals' lives. We recommend this approach only if you write, speak, or blog fairly often.

Our management consultant friend mentioned in the preceding sidebar knew that the *New York Times* was too formidable an institution to be likely to honor a request from her to remove the wedding announcement, so she didn't even try the "wash it out" approach. Her only realistic options were to take active steps online to bury the content under more brand-relevant information (wash over it) or just let it get buried eventually without taking any action—the "wait it out" method.

She decided not to take any active steps to bury the wedding announcement and instead took the "wait it out" approach. As a published author and active member of her professional community, she was likely to have more online content developed about her even without her intervention. Plus, the dirt was merely distracting, not damaging, so she wasn't in a huge hurry to bury the wedding announcement. Sure enough, the "wait it out" method worked. Within a couple of months, she Googled herself again and found that five new search results topped the list over her wedding announcement without her having done anything. (The results were related to some new sites listing her books for sale.)

Calling in the Pros to Clean Up Your Digital Dirt

In recent years, many consumers have subscribed to services that monitor the security of their personal financial credit to protect against identity theft or other inappropriate uses of their credit. It only makes sense, then, that you can now employ the services—for a fee, of course—of businesses that will keep an eye on your online reputation and help you keep it clean.

(continued)

(continued)

> One of the pioneers in this field, ReputationDefender (www.
> reputationdefender.com), goes on a search-and-destroy mission. This organi-
> zation scours the Internet to dig up every bit of information on you and
> then sets out to destroy (at your request) any negative information by
> getting it corrected or removed, whenever possible.

Whichever method you choose to bury or eradicate your digital dirt, be patient because it might take time to achieve your desired results.

Defining Your Online Identity

> **Tip:** *For more help with assessing your online identity and cleaning up your digital dirt, turn to personal branding experts William Arruda and Kirsten Dixson at www.careerdistinction.com.*

Our local chapter of the national organization ExecuNet holds networking meetings twice a month that attract six-figure job seekers, recruiters, and entrepreneurs, as well as executives who simply like to stay connected even when they're not in job search mode. Each meeting features an informative speaker and some mingling time over hors d'oeuvres and soft drinks, as well as a block of time for every attendee to stand at the front of the room and give his or her "elevator speech"—a one- or two-minute pitch that provides an overview of his or her background and goals. Borrowing a term coined by author Michelle Tullier in *Networking for Job Search and Career Success* (JIST, 2004), we call this your "self-marketing sound bite"—a quick synopsis of who you are, what you've done, what you have to offer, and what you're looking for.

We've been speakers and participants at these meetings and always find that only a handful of the participants' self-marketing sound bites stand out as memorable. The rest tend to sound too much like everyone else's. They're usually a recitation of work history chronology and some vague comments about goals—nothing disastrous, just not very distinctive.

> *"From time to time, I read blog posts or comments that state or imply that cultivating a personal brand is about shameless self promotion. Arguably, if you look at the very strong brands of some of the executives and celebrities of our time, it sure can seem that way.*

"And yet, having, cultivating, and even promoting a personal brand is anything but a shameless ego trip. It is really about using your strengths and your passions to make a difference for other people."

—from the blog of Walter Akana, www.threshold-consulting.com

Whether you're a six-figure executive or someone just looking for a paycheck that'll cover the rent, you have to develop the habit of speaking about yourself in a way that will make you stand out from the pack—that will establish your personal brand in the minds of others.

Making an effort to be visible and memorable is even more important when you're networking online. You have to rely on the written word to get your message across rather than body language, tone of voice, or attire. Your words must pack a punch. What can make your message memorable? We recommend five strategies:

1. Tout the benefits, not the features.

2. Be clear and concise.

3. Be unique.

4. Show your personality.

5. Be consistent and persistent.

Tout the Benefits, Not the Features

Take a tip from tried-and-true advertising strategies and don't give the details of your work history or a laundry list of degrees and credentials. Instead, give a few key highlights of your experience, accomplishments, and contributions. It's like a cereal box telling consumers that the contents will help lower their cholesterol without getting into the food chemistry behind why that will happen. People who are going to hire, network, or do business with you don't need to know every detail of your history. They just need to know what you've done for others and what you can do for them. If they really do want or need the details, they can always read your resume or Web site later.

> **Tip:** *Not sure how to articulate the benefits you offer? Take stock of your skills and positive personal qualities by completing quick self-directed assessment exercises or formal testing through a career coach. Links to sites that offer do-it-yourself assessments and information on the coach-led ones are provided in the appendix of this book.*

Be Clear and Concise

When you network with someone, you're not only telling that person about yourself, but also hoping that this one networking contact will spread the word to others about who you are and what you have to offer. Whether you meet with individuals one-on-one or in a group setting, you are in essence training those people to be your sales force. They are going to go out and spread the word about you and your needs, goals, talents, or services.

Of course, when networking online, you reach a larger number of people more quickly, so if each of those connections tells a friend, who tells a friend, who tells a friend…well, you get the picture. The viral marketing quality of networking has the power to do great things for you, but only if the message that is being spread about you is the one that you want spread. It is critical, therefore, that every message you share about yourself be clear, concise, and easy to understand. Networking this way is like training that sales force to go out and market a product. They won't be successful if they don't have a solid understanding of the product and some language to use when talking about it.

Be Unique

Our editor for this book, who has also been a career counselor for many years, has an interesting tidbit of information that she almost always includes when speaking about her background. A few years ago, she was invited jointly by the United States Department of State and the King of Jordan to spend a few weeks in Jordan helping that country's universities establish or improve their career counseling departments. Since then, when she has to give a brief overview of her experience and credentials, she often mentions that experience, even though it is actually not directly relevant to her current career emphasis and goals. (She operates more in corporate than academic arenas now.) It's unique and interesting, though, so it makes her self-marketing sound bite stick in people's minds. And it establishes her brand as a subject matter expert with an international flair.

> **Tip:** When you're networking online, your self-marketing sound bite will typically be delivered in writing rather than being spoken. To make sure it is clear, easily understood, and quick to read, ask some friends and colleagues to test-drive it for you. Have them read your self-marketing sound bite and give you feedback on what they glean from it and how long they took to read it.

Think about what makes you unique or different. What adds color and interest to your pitch? It doesn't have to involve high levels of government or royalty! Anything that is a little out of the ordinary will work, whether it's a special project, an especially impressive accomplishment, or anything else that is likely to make you more memorable.

Show Your Personality

Let your personality show through in all you do when connecting with others online. Unless you're interacting with people live through a podcast (a live audio broadcast like a radio program but via the Internet) or other voice connection, your message will be delivered online in a fairly static, one-dimensional fashion. People will get to know you through your profile statement on a social network, through the bio on your Web site, or through comments on blogs or discussion groups.

In online networking, people have to get to know you through your written words. They won't see your confident body language or animated facial expressions. They won't feel your firm handshake or sense the energy in your voice. You have to find a way to let your personality, energy, and enthusiasm shine through. This can be done by writing as if you were speaking directly to the reader, using humor where appropriate, and expressing opinions (as long as they are relevant to the topic at hand and won't get you into trouble!).

> **Tip:** To keep an eye on when, where, and how you appear online, set up a Google Alert (www.google.com/alerts). With a Google Alert, you receive updates by e-mail of new content on the Web that relates to a topic you've requested. That topic should be you, of course. To set it up, enter your name as the search term and select whether you want to receive updates once a day, once a week, or as they happen.

Be Consistent and Persistent

A message heard once is not likely to be remembered or acted upon. If you know anything about advertising, you know that placing an advertisement once is usually not sufficient. Media campaigns involve repeated placements of ads over time, and often in multiple media sources, such as newspapers, magazines, Web sites, and maybe even television or radio.

If you are marketing yourself for a job or for career advancement or business development, you need to have a multipronged approach to getting out the word about you and what you have to offer. In chapter 3, you'll learn more about the various online avenues for gaining professional visibility and can start to select the best ones for you.

The Goals of a Self-Marketing Sound Bite

The term "elevator speech" is based on the notion that if you find yourself riding on an elevator with someone who could be valuable to your career or business, you should be able to communicate your selling points by the time that person gets off the elevator. A self-marketing sound bite is a form of elevator pitch. It's a brief statement that conveys who you are and what you have to offer. It's a concise statement that, when posted as online content, should take someone anywhere from 15 to 30 seconds to read.

You'll use your self-marketing sound bite as the foundation for the profiles you'll post online as well as when e-mailing people or conversing in chat rooms. A good self-marketing sound bite hits the highlights of who you are, what you've done, and what you or your business has to offer. It conveys your personal brand and online identity. Your sound bite should do four main things:

- Put yourself on the map.

- Pitch your strengths.

- Back up your claims with evidence.

- State what you're looking for.

Putting Yourself on the Map

Putting yourself on the map means establishing who you are in terms of your work or educational status, situation, and roles. That might include your job title, career area, functional role(s), and an overview of your experience or your business offerings and background.

Examples:

> I have 15 years of experience in software sales, including 5 years in sales management roles.

I'm a physical therapist specializing in sports injuries.

I'm a junior at Georgia Tech majoring in civil engineering and have held internships with Garrett Construction and in city government.

As an independent consultant for the past several years, I've helped more than 50 small businesses gain market share and grow their revenues through cost-effective local marketing efforts.

> **Tip:** *Remember that your self-marketing sound bite is a building block for profiles you post on social networking sites or for your bio on a webfolio or blog, so it will be out there for all the world to see—literally. Protect your privacy by not including personal data such as your address, phone number, Social Security number, or tax ID number.*

Pitching Your Strengths

When pitching your strengths, you mention the positive points that will help you reach your goals. These points may cover the categories described next.

Skills

Don't give a laundry list of skills, but cite two or three examples. Remember that the exercises and tests on the sites listed in the appendix can help you come up with your top skills if you don't already know them off the top of your head.

Examples:

I am fluent in Mandarin and Russian, both written and spoken.

I am highly proficient in Excel and PowerPoint.

My particular talent is in turnaround situations, winning back business from dissatisfied clients and driving growth and revenue.

Areas of Expertise

Think about what you have to know to do your job or be successful in your business. This is your content knowledge or subject matter expertise.

Examples:

> I'm a human resources generalist with in-depth knowledge of compensation and benefits.

> My interdisciplinary major exposed me to many current issues in education and public policy.

Personal Qualities

What distinguishes you from others you've worked with or other businesses in your market?

Examples:

> My managers have always commented on my initiative and strong work ethic.

> I'm known as a resourceful problem-solver.

> My clients appreciate my ability as a consultant to get at the heart of their needs quickly and develop cost-effective solutions.

Backing Up Your Claims

Making claims about what you can do is one thing. It's another to provide evidence of what you have done. You therefore should include a very brief mention of one of your achievements as part of your self-marketing sound bite. Remember, be brief. You can always elaborate more later if someone is interested in hearing the whole story. Note that the best achievement statements include both the actions or effort taken as well as the positive outcome. In other words, don't just say what you achieved; tell how you did it.

Sample Achievement Statements:

> I reduced accident incidents on the plant floor by 32 percent in a 12-month period by developing and implementing new safety procedures.

After taking over a call center that was getting too many customer complaints and had been operating over budget for the past year, I streamlined operations to reduce expenses by 40 percent and enhanced training programs to improve customer feedback ratings by 20 percent.

As president of my homeowner's association, I spearheaded improvements that led to an equity increase of $1.5 million across the 120 homes, which was a much higher rate of increase than that of surrounding subdivisions.

My consulting firm recently helped a client identify $6,000 per month in operating cost savings opportunities by hiring us for a process re-engineering engagement.

To help you develop your achievement statements, pull out past performance reviews; logs you may have kept of successes at work; project files; letters of praise from bosses, colleagues, or customers; and anything else that will help you remember what you've contributed to your employers or clients. You might also have included examples of accomplishments in your resume, so refer to your current or past resumes for ideas as well.

What Have You Done for Us Lately?

To develop your achievement statements, ask yourself the following questions to jog your memory about noteworthy things you've done. Don't worry if not all apply to you; just try to find a few that help you come up with achievements you can talk about in your networking. Write examples on the lines that follow each question.

Did I save an employer or client money?

_____

_____

_____

(continued)

(continued)

Did I help an employer or client make more money?

_____

_____

_____

Have I done something in a new and better way? Developed a new system or process? Been innovative and creative?

_____

_____

_____

Have I received any awards or special recognition?

_____

_____

_____

Am I known for being particularly good at something that distinguishes me from my peers? Am I relied upon as the go-to person for something?

_____

_____

_____

Have there been particularly challenging situations in which I've excelled?

_____

_____

_____

Did I ever take on extra work or a special project that wasn't part of my regular role?

_____

What am I the most proud of in my professional and/or civic life?

Telling Them What You Want

A final component of your sound bite is to clarify what you want or need. If you're looking for a job, you would briefly state why you are in the market and what jobs you're targeting. If you're seeking career management or advancement advice, give a concise description of where you are in your career and why you're seeking help. If you have your own business, indicate the types of customers, clients, or referrals that are appropriate for you.

For example:

> I'm hoping to expand my eldercare business into the southwestern United States and would like to learn more about the assisted-living market in that region.

> **Tip:** *Your self-marketing sound bite is all about you, you, you! Don't forget, though, that genuine networking is about giving to others as much as you ask them to give to you. Talking about what you need is okay, but also make sure that you ask others how you can help them.*

> My position with XYZ Company was eliminated as part of a major reduction-in-force, and I'm now looking for a position as a marketing manager in a mid-sized company in the banking or finance industry.

If you're not currently looking for a new job or actively seeking to develop new business, you don't have to include the "tell them what you want" section of your sound bite. You might instead offer simply a value contribution statement that tells people what you can do for them. A financial advisor, for example, might say something like

> I help my clients shave years off their retirement target date.

A software salesperson might say

> I make money by helping you save money. I offer cost-effective software solutions that will improve your operating efficiencies and cut costs.

Developing Your Self-Marketing Sound Bite

To make it easy for you to construct a self-marketing sound bite, we've provided the following template. All you have to do is fill in the blanks to customize a sound bite for yourself. Keep in mind, though, that using a template like this doesn't allow much room for originality. Feel free to mix up the order, jazz up the wording, and make the message your own. This template should serve only as a basic guide to help you start; then you can be creative and let the real you show through.

JOB SEEKER TEMPLATE

With _____ years of experience in the _____ industry, I've developed expertise in _____ and _____. I've held roles in/as _____ [put your functional areas or titles here], and most recently have been [or currently am] a _____ [current or most recent functional role or title goes here] with _____ [current or most recent employer name goes here].

Within _____ [overall functional area, for example, marketing, sales, public administration], I have special expertise in _____ and _____. Recently, for example, I _____ [accomplishment example goes here].

Throughout my career, I've gained a reputation for _____ [skills and personal qualities]. My work experience is complemented by _____ [educational degree, certifications/licenses, or other relevant credentials].

I'm seeking a _____ [type of position sought] in
_____ [target industry or type of employer].

Following is a sample self-marketing sound bite for a job seeker:

> With more than 20 years of experience in banking, I've demonstrated a consistent track record of growing market share and generating revenue. I've held a variety of progressively responsible roles in marketing and client relations and most recently was Vice President of Client Services with Regional Bank.
>
> I have special expertise in using Web-based solutions for customer acquisition and retention. Recently, for example, I was recognized with our Chairman's Award for the most outstanding contribution to the organization last year for leading my team to develop Internet marketing strategies that broke the mold.
>
> Throughout my career I've been known for my innovative but practical solutions to challenging business retention and development issues.
>
> I'm now seeking a leadership role in a community bank with an entrepreneurial environment where I can contribute my talents and experience for rapid growth and profitability.

Not Job Seeking? Sound Bites for the Rest of Us

If you're not actively looking for a job but simply want to enhance how you do business, whether you're employed in an organization or self-employed, you still need a self-marketing sound bite. It will enable you to convey to people who you are and what you have to offer so that you can attract the right kinds of people to network with—people with whom you can share ideas, knowledge, leads, and referrals.

You can use many components of the job seekers' sound bite, including the overview of your experience, skills or personal qualities, and contribution highlights, but you just don't have to get into what you're looking for.

Here's a sample all-purpose self-marketing sound bite:

> Over the past 12 years I've developed a solid track record in sales management, consistently leading teams that exceed revenue plans and expand market share. I've become known as "the turnaround guy"—someone who can win back accounts that are on the rocks and get business units back to profitability.
>
> I began my career with XYZ Corporation, where I was an outside sales rep for three years before promotion into management. From there, I held sales leadership roles with increasingly larger territories and responsibilities in the chemicals and pharmaceutical industries.
>
> I'm currently vice president of a nine-state region for QRS Corporation and serve on the board of directors for IJK Foundation.

Now that you have a sense of how important your online steps are to projecting your professional brand to the world and how to start going about doing so, you're ready to develop a plan for exactly where to go online and how much time to spend there. Chapter 3 walks you through the process of targeting the best ways for you to network online.

Key Points: Chapter 2

- Having an online identity is becoming increasingly important as a way to establish your credibility and personal brand and to attract career or business opportunities.

- The first step in establishing your online identity is to Google yourself and assess how strong your "digital footprint" is and whether it conveys positive information about you.

- You have three choices for dealing with negative online information about yourself: replace it with more positive content, have it removed, or wait it out and let new content appear over it.

- To communicate your personal brand online, develop a self-marketing sound bite—a brief statement that conveys who you are and what you have to offer.

Chapter 3

Seven Ways to Network Online: A Technology for Every Day of the Week

So many choices, so little time. That's a common lament of online networkers. Like any activity on the Internet, connecting with people virtually and maintaining an online identity can be major time-eaters. You therefore need to be focused in your efforts and realistic about what you can accomplish on a daily or weekly basis. That means having a solid handle on what's involved in the various online networking technologies and understanding which ones are the best fit for your particular situation.

In this chapter, we first help you identify your goals—what you aim to accomplish through networking online. Then we survey the seven main categories of Web-based networking technologies so that you can start to decide where to devote your time (and sometimes your money) to yield the best return on investment.

In This Chapter

- Identify your online networking goals.
- Complement your traditional (offline) networking efforts.
- Learn which online networking avenues are best for reaching your goals.

Knowledge Breeds Success

You have to know what you're getting into when you network online. You can think of this as the old "look before you leap" advice. Some networking avenues require significant start-up time and money but minimal ongoing maintenance, whereas others are easy and cheap to dive into but require constant care and feeding.

You might start out in some of the more high-maintenance networking activities with the best of intentions, but like dieting, exercising, and cleaning out the garage, unless you commit to keeping up your efforts long term, you won't achieve much success. Starting a blog that you don't keep active, for example, is more damaging to your professional image than not having one at all. Similarly, putting a profile on LinkedIn is a good first step, but unless you take the time to invite people to join your network or accept invitations to others' networks, you're not actively participating.

So let's start by identifying your networking goals and then learn what's involved in the various online networking technologies.

Identifying Your Online Networking Goals

Networking should be a part of every professional's or business owner's life on an ongoing, "don't-even-have-to-think-about-it" basis. Having a large network of quality people to turn to for assistance at a moment's notice is critical for success. And having a range of people who can turn to you for support as they strive to reach their goals is highly rewarding. So, in some sense, your networking goal should be very broad: Just do it! You never know when you'll need to call upon a contact to help you out or when you will have the opportunity to get satisfaction out of helping someone else.

Nevertheless, there are times in the life of a career or business when networking—both offline and online—needs to be a more concentrated effort. You might need a new job or advice on getting a raise or promotion. Or maybe you need to lift your business out of the doldrums and generate more sales and revenue. Whatever the reason, there is an online networking avenue that can help you solve your problems and achieve your objectives.

Don't Do It Just Because We Said So!

If you're a job seeker, don't network online simply because a career coach told you to. Do it because you have specific employment goals in mind and know that networking on the Internet will help you reach your targets.

If you're a recruiter or employer seeking candidates, don't network online simply because you hear that lots of your colleagues are on business-oriented social networks such as LinkedIn or Ecademy. Identify the types of candidates or corporate clients you're seeking and see if those or other online forums are the best sources of those targets.

And, if you are networking online to develop business or make sales, don't do it just to jump on the bandwagon. Do it because you know that online tools can help you drum up leads and intelligence on your prospects.

Let's look at some of the specific goals you might have, depending on your situation.

Online Networking Goals for Job Seekers

Depending on whose survey results you believe—and many such surveys are conducted every year—75 to 85 percent of jobs typically are found through networking. Connecting with people who can lead you to potential employers—or attracting the right people through your professional visibility—is usually the most effective job search method for most people.

Now, with online networking avenues to complement your in-person, offline networking efforts, you have more chances than ever of landing a position through connections you make.

In the mid- to late-1990s, online job boards revolutionized job search. No longer did job seekers have to scour the newspaper and then mail or fax resumes and cover letters in response to advertisements for jobs. They could browse hundreds of thousands of job postings online through sites such as Monster and many others. And, with the click of a few buttons, they could put their resumes in front of recruiters and employers.

This capability was especially helpful when people were searching for jobs long distance. No more trying to dig up an out-of-town newspaper or going to the expense of spending days in another city pounding the pavement to knock on employers' doors. Internet-based job hunting opened global doors from the convenience of one's own home.

It's About People, Not Postings

Don't confuse online networking with using online job boards. Sites such as Monster, CareerBuilder, and many more still play a vital role in identifying employment opportunities through the job postings they offer. But uploading your resume to a job site or applying for positions through those sites is not online networking. It's simply applying for jobs. Online networking is the process of getting to know real people or making yourself visible so that real people get to know you.

A Bona Fide Job Search Revolution!

A major transformation has not come along in the world of job search in a dozen years, but recently, online networking has been just that. It has transformed how people who need jobs connect with people who have jobs or with people who know of people who have jobs. Maybe we need to get a life, but as career counselors who coach job seekers every day, we find this development incredibly exciting and hope you will as well.

Job Seekers: What Do *You* Want to Accomplish Online?

Through Internet-based networking avenues, you, as a job hunter, can accomplish everything that you would in offline networking. Online networking helps at all phases of your search. Some specific goals you might have include the following:

- Advice on determining your specific career or job objective

- Information about industries, fields, and occupations you are targeting in your search or considering targeting

- Strategic advice about your self-marketing plan and approach to your search

- Input on the tools of your search, such as feedback on your resume, cover letters, self-marketing sound bite, and more

- Suggestions of general types of employers or recruiters to target, as well as names of specific organizations or search firms to approach

- Insight into the culture, strengths and weaknesses, hiring methods, or other characteristics of organizations you are targeting for employment

- Names of people to contact to learn about actual employment opportunities

- Direct leads to job openings

- Advice on evaluating and negotiating job offers

- Emotional support through the ups and downs of your search

Later in this chapter you learn about specific networking avenues that can help you reach any or all these goals. But, no matter which online networking path you choose to follow, the important thing is simply to do it.

Make it a part of your search as you would working with recruiters, sending out resumes and cover letters, attending job fairs, and applying to positions online.

Online Networking Really Is Worth the Time

As career coaches, we often find that it's a struggle to convince job seekers that networking is worth the time and effort. We know it's so much easier to sit at your computer and fire off resumes in reply to job postings. But would you rather do that for months on end or cut down your job search time considerably by networking your way to a job? With online networking, you now have the best of both worlds. You can do it from the convenience of your office or plopped on the couch with your laptop, and it still counts as networking! So there really are no excuses for not networking in a job search.

Online Networking Goals for Managing Your Career

Even if you're not actively searching for a new job, you ought to network anyway. Staying visible in your professional community and maintaining a solid network of business relationships are key to career satisfaction and success. Think of networking as "taking a village to raise a career." Sure, you—and only you—are ultimately responsible for steering your career where you want it to go, but having an army of allies at your disposal doesn't hurt.

Networking online can be an asset throughout the entire life cycle of your career, from becoming established, to advancing or changing roles in your organization or career field, to deciding when to scale back toward retirement. Some specific goals you might have for your online networking include the following:

- Enhance your job performance and productivity by learning best practices for innovation, creativity, and efficiency. This knowledge can come from people in your field as well as those in other industries or professions who might have a fresh perspective for you.

- Position yourself for promotions, advancement, and raises by being more savvy about your field and your role and by getting strategic negotiating advice from people in your network.

- Keep an eye on the competition—know what other organizations in your market are up to.

- Get more familiar with your customer or client base, vendors, suppliers, or any other constituencies that you and your employer buy from, sell to, or serve.

- Be on the lookout for opportunities for a career change or job change, just in case the grass might be greener somewhere else.

- Position yourself as a passive job candidate, someone who is not actively searching but can be found online by recruiters and employers if the perfect opportunity comes up.

- Feel connected to your professional community at-large and gain a sense of collegiality.

- Get ideas for semi-retirement career options and ways to start to phase out your full-time career.

Whether you're at the entry level of your career or well established, online networking can enhance your satisfaction and success. It helps you make sure that where you are is where you want to be. And, if you're not where you want to be, it helps you get there.

Online Networking Goals for Recruiters

As we mentioned in chapter 1, recruiters as a whole have a reputation for being expert networkers. Their success depends largely on making word-of-mouth connections to find the right people for the right jobs. It's no surprise, then, that recruiters have embraced online networking, particularly social networking sites such as LinkedIn, as a way to pump up their networking efforts and dig even deeper and more widely for qualified candidates and lucrative clients.

Whether you're a contingency staffing recruiter or a highly specialized executive search consultant, online networking can greatly enhance your business. Specific goals you might have include the following:

- Sourcing candidates, including those hard-to-find ones buried deep in an organization or those who aren't actively looking

- Prescreening candidates by checking out their credentials online and finding out whether they have "digital dirt"

- Developing business—that is, securing more client companies whose search needs you can fulfill

- Gaining insight into the needs, culture, structure, and business goals of your clients or targeted clients

- Finding potential partners to collaborate with, such as arranging split-fee business with other recruiters

Many recruiters are already reaching these goals by being on social network sites, but there's much more to online networking than LinkedIn. Blogging or reading others' blogs and participating in discussion groups are also ways to attain these goals.

Online Networking Goals for Business Owners and Business Developers

Developing business for your own entrepreneurial endeavor or as a sales or marketing professional is more than placing ads and making cold calls. People like to do business with people they know, so networking is critical for business owners and salespeople.

Networking online helps with all aspects of running and growing a business or making sales. Typical goals include the following:

- Help with making the decision to go into business for yourself

- Strategic advice about structuring and launching your business or a particular product, including writing the business plan or marketing materials and hiring staff

- Referral sources of customers or clients

- Connections to actual customers or clients

- Sourcing strategic alliance partners or employees

- A sense of connection to a larger community—a sort of virtual team of coworkers for a small or solo business

- Information on possible vendors or suppliers for the business

- The ability to keep an eye on the competition

- Insight into the needs, culture, quirks, and other characteristics of your target customers or clients

- Virtual marketing options for launching or expanding the business or product lines

- Emotional support through the ups and downs of starting and running a business or closing deals

Entrepreneurs and salespeople often feel too busy to do Internet-based networking—or so they think.

Salespeople are usually on the go, calling on clients, wining and dining prospective clients, or attending in-person networking events. Rarely are they found sitting in front of a computer, at least not by choice. Similarly, entrepreneurs are usually not tied to a desk. They're pulled in many different directions to run all aspects of the business.

We're not saying that any of those things should stop. We simply recommend adding online networking to your business development arsenal. You might actually find that you save time because of the shortcuts it offers for reaching more people, more quickly.

WORKSHEET: MY ONLINE NETWORKING GOALS

Now that you have a sense of the many possible goals that you can attain through networking online, it's time to put on paper the specific goals you want to reach. You can do so by answering the following questions, either here in the book or by creating your own form on paper or electronically.

1. What is my top-priority goal?

This is the big-picture goal. It might be long term or fairly near term.

Example: I want to land a job in an organization that is more family-friendly.

Example: I want to develop new business among midsized companies in the pharmaceutical industry.

Now write a few lines about your goal:

_____

_____

_____

_____

---

2. What are some specific objectives or milestones that will help me reach that goal?

These are specific things you need to reach your goal. Skimming over the preceding lists can provide ideas.

Example: Identifying companies in my geographic area that are family-friendly. Finding people who have insight into the culture of, and possible opportunities at, certain family-friendly companies I am already considering.

Example: Getting to know five people this week who work in mid-sized pharmaceutical companies.

_____

_____

_____

_____

3. Who can help me reach my goals and objectives?

Your reply here should include categories of people who might be able to help you move closer to your goals. For example, the person with a goal of developing new business in the pharmaceutical industry might need to connect with scientists or people in companies that make the equipment used in pharmaceutical labs. The family-oriented job seeker might want to connect with people who congregate in online parenting forums.

_____

_____

_____

_____

Online Networking Can Pick Up the Slack Where Offline Networking Falls Short

As you start to think about how you're going to use online networking to reach the goals you've identified, first consider what you're already doing in the way of traditional networking and think about the quality and quantity of your network itself. Consider these questions:

- How large and strong is your network? How many of those people do you have solid business relationships with, as opposed to having nothing more than contact names in a database—people you barely know?

- How well rounded is your network? Are your contacts spread across industries and organizations, or clustered in one organization you've worked for or within one industry or professional field?

- How geographically disbursed is your network? Are there certain locations where you could benefit from knowing more people?

- What roles do the people in your network fulfill? Are they mostly referral sources of business or primarily coworkers and former work colleagues? Are they more personal contacts than professional?

Developing a Full-Service Network

To make sure that you have someone to turn to for every need that might arise as you strive toward your professional and business goals, consider how well rounded your network is. A good model for this is the "STARS" system, developed by career consultant Michelle Tullier and described in detail in her book *Networking for Job Search and Career Success* (JIST, 2004). She defines a well-balanced network as one that includes relationships with people who can play the following roles in your career or business development:

- **S**trategists: The people who help you plot a course toward your goals. They give advice, feedback, and coaching to direct you down the right path.

- **T**argets: The people most closely linked to your career or business goals—the people you've set your sights on reaching, such as prospective employers, customers, or clients.

- **A**llied forces: The professionals who provide expertise to strengthen your networking efforts and brand expression. They might be image consultants, Web site designers, career coaches, communications consultants, and more.

- **R**ole models: The mentors or sages who serve as role models for your business or career and who can offer advice and wisdom.

- **S**upporters: The people who provide emotional support and cheer you along the path to reaching your goals.

Do you need more stars in your network? If so, online networking might be the answer to developing not just a larger network, but a more "full-service" one.

In the next section, you learn more about the various online networking options and start to see how they can help you reach the goals and objectives you've defined.

Where in the Virtual World Will You Network?

You probably know by now that accomplishing anything on the Internet means being a wise consumer and making good choices. If you've ever planned a vacation or booked a business flight online, you probably had to choose between using Expedia, Orbitz, or Travelocity. Or maybe you went straight to an airline's own site or through a travel agency with an online presence. Bottom line is that you had more than enough choices to get the information you needed and make the transaction.

The process of online networking is not all that different. Most Web-based networking options fall into a handful of main categories, such as social networks, blogs, Web sites, and discussion forums. But there are usually several popular choices in each category, as well as many less "household-name" choices.

In this section, we briefly define each of the main online networking technologies to help you start thinking about which ones are the best fit for you and your goals and needs. Then, in chapters 4, 5, and 6, we elaborate on these networking avenues to deepen your understanding of them, explore the pros and cons, and walk you through the how-tos.

The seven main categories described here are as follows:

- Social networks

- Identity management sites

- Blogs

- Webfolios
- Discussion groups
- Online publishing
- Online public speaking

There are many ways to slice the online networking pie into categories, so we don't claim that our way is the only way. For example, webfolios and blogs often overlap, and blogging is a form of publishing, but looking at the options in terms of these seven categories will help you start to navigate your way through the options to zero in on the ones that will work best for you.

1. Social Networks

Picture yourself in a large convention hall with thousands of business cards flying through the air like confetti. Imagine yourself struggling to make your way through the crowds and the "confetti" to meet the right people. Suddenly, you come upon a trusted business colleague or former classmate who takes you by the hand and introduces you to someone who, in turn, leads you to a person you need to meet. Dream or reality? With online, business-oriented social networks, this is more reality than dream.

How Social Networks Work

Social networks such as LinkedIn, Ecademy, XING, and many others help people connect with each other to do business, make career moves, and advance professionally. In chapter 4 we go into much more detail about social networks—how they operate and how to use them—but here we want to introduce you to the concept and help you start to see whether social networking is for you.

On these sites, you build a network by first posting a profile—basically a bio and other information about yourself and your professional interests—and then invite other people to join your network. You can also accept invitations from other members, thereby linking their networks to yours. Membership in these networks is typically free, or you can pay a nominal fee for an upgraded membership that offers added benefits—namely, greater access to the membership at-large.

Who Social Networks Are For

Just about anyone can benefit from joining a business-oriented social network. Job seekers secure interviews and land jobs through them, recruiters find qualified candidates, and business owners or business developers broaden their referral bases and find key players in their targeted customer organizations.

Membership in a social network requires minimal technical and writing skills. This membership is easy to maintain.

2. Identity Management Sites

Across a very blurry line from the business-oriented social networks are the sites that we call identity management sites. They're also known as profile management sites and even as reputation builders. On these sites, you post your profile as a way for people to find information about you when they do a keyword search for you online. Some of these sites also offer ways for you to connect with other members, so they are similar to social networks, thus the blurry line.

How Identity Management Sites Work

Most sites offer profile placement free, but on some you can upgrade your membership for a nominal fee. This upgrade gives you premium placement status, meaning that when someone searches for you on major search engines such as Google, your profile will come up at the top of the page.

The profile you post is much like one you would put on LinkedIn or Ecademy. It's basically a bio with an overview of your professional background, with the option to include some bells and whistles such as a photo or links to your own blog or Web site.

> **Tip:** Sites like Ziggs and Naymz are especially helpful if your name is not unique and you want to establish your identity online under a variation of your name, such as by including your middle initial or full maiden name. You can start to build up a digital footprint under that name by using it when you join these sites.

Two of the most popular sites in this category are Naymz and Ziggs. Naymz describes itself as an "innovative reputation network" that lets you establish and promote your name online. Ziggs calls itself a "one-stop source for creating and managing your online brand." The benefit of both sites is that you can gain some control over your digital identity by ensuring that at least one Google hit for your name (or two, if you join both sites) will have accurate, up-to-date information about you. Of course, you have to manage your profile to keep it up-to-date and accurate.

Who Can Benefit from Identity Management Sites

Identity management sites are easy to use, quick to join and set up, free (or inexpensive for upgraded membership), and require minimal ongoing maintenance, so they are good for just about everyone. They also require minimal writing and technology skills. (Just be sure to get some help writing and proofreading your profile if you're not a good writer.) These sites are especially useful for anyone who has little to no online presence and needs to start developing a digital footprint.

There's very little downside to these sites because they require minimal output of effort, skill, or money.

3. Blogs

Blogs—shorthand for *web logs*—are one of the most significant developments in the history of the Internet. In recent years, the Web morphed from a purveyor of fairly static, online content to a forum for interaction and dialogue. The Internet became not just a place to read about stuff, but a place to have a conversation—or more likely, many conversations.

How Blogs Work

If you're already familiar with blogs—maybe you have your own or have commented on other people's—then you know that blogs come in all shapes and sizes. Some have been active for years and are rich in content. Many posts and comments have been archived over time, so you can catch up on past discussions. Some are frequently updated with fresh postings on a daily or at least weekly basis. Others have less activity. Maybe they are newer or just have fewer, less frequent postings and a smaller audience.

Whichever shape and size a blog takes on, it is an excellent vehicle for expression of a personal brand and establishment of a digital trail. If you write a comment on a popular blog, you will make a mark that will be picked up by the major search engines. If you have your own blog and post on it regularly, you will see references to your blog come up when anyone Googles your name.

A Few of Our Favorite Blogs

1. Force_of_Good by Lance Weatherby: http://blog.weatherby.net
2. JibberJobber by Jason Alba: www.jibberjobber.com/blog/
3. Threshold Consulting—It's Your Life, Own It! by Walter Akana: http://walterakana.typepad.com/

Who Can Benefit from Blogging

Just about anyone can benefit from blogging. Commenting on other people's blogs is free, and setting up your own is quick, easy, and inexpensive. Of course, you do need to have some degree of writing skill and like to write, but if you comment on others' blogs rather than having your own, minimal skill is needed.

Commenting on blogs is especially helpful for job seekers. Your blog comments are likely to turn up high in a list of Google hits for your name, and it's a great way to show off your expertise and thought process. Having your own blog might be worth the effort if you are an entrepreneur who needs the visibility for marketing purposes or if you're a professional looking to make a mark in his or her professional world.

4. Webfolios: The Resume That Works While You Sleep

One of the earliest ways that job seekers and other professionals could create visibility for themselves online was to develop a personal Web site, often called a webfolio. Much like a literal portfolio—a notebook, binder, or folder you might carry to showcase your experience, qualifications, and work samples—a webfolio tells people who you are and what you've done. It just happens to be entirely electronic and housed on the Internet.

Webfolios are not as popular as they once were, now that blogs have made the Web more interactive. Blogs enable an individual to be more visible and develop relationships with more people than is often possible with a webfolio that has static, read-only content. But webfolios still have their place.

Webfolios are great for active job seekers. They bring a paper resume to life. They are also an asset for passive job seekers—professionals who are not actively on the market but wouldn't mind attracting employers or recruiters who might have appealing opportunities to present. They can also be useful for people who have little interest in changing jobs but simply need a sort of online brochure about themselves—a place to direct people who might be interested in working with them in some capacity.

A webfolio is easy to maintain. You do need to keep it up-to-date with fresh information about yourself and make it interesting for visitors with articles or links to other sites. But a webfolio is not as dynamic as a blog, so the expectation is that you will update it only occasionally and not necessarily on a daily or weekly basis.

> **Tip:** *In most cases, the URL (Internet address) of your webfolio should be the same as your name, or something close to your name. The site is not so much for the purpose of promoting a business you own or an organization you work for as it is simply your online professional calling card—a place for people to learn who you are.*

5. Discussion Groups

Long before blogging technology came into existence, people were communicating on the Internet through various forums. Like a virtual water cooler, discussion groups and other online forums have enabled people with common interests to form communities for sharing ideas, opinions, advice, and best practices in their fields.

Yahoo! and Google are credited with having some of the most extensive offerings of special-interest discussion groups online, although many lesser known organizations have them as well. In these discussion groups, participants post comments or questions in a sort of virtual bulletin board or message board format, and others post replies or rebuttals.

With discussion groups, unlike chat rooms and instant messaging, you can log on at any time to post or read others' posts; the exchanges are not live in real time. This format can be quite convenient. As with reading e-mail, you can do it whenever you feel like it. And even without real-time, live exchanges, you can form surprisingly strong bonds with fellow group members. Discussion groups can be a great way to express your brand because you are able to demonstrate your knowledge and expertise.

> **Tip:** *Some discussion groups might have people who meet locally offline, that is, in person. Check to see if any discussion group you participate in has live meetings somewhere convenient so that you can transition from online networking to offline.*

6. Online Publishing

When you think of the networking process, writing for publication probably isn't the first thing that comes to mind. It doesn't seem as interactive as meeting someone for coffee or mingling at a professional conference. But, in fact, writing for professional publications has always been one of the best-kept secrets of networking.

Writing articles, editorials, and book or product reviews for professional newsletters and journals, trade publications, and popular media is an excellent way to express your personal brand and gain visibility. Remember that networking isn't just about going out and meeting other people; it's also about attracting people to you through activities you become involved with, leadership you exhibit, and good works you do.

The Internet has opened the door for just about everyone to get published. If you can't get your writing accepted in prestigious journals, you can start your own blog or e-newsletter (an electronic newsletter that you e-mail to subscribers) and become an instant author.

Okay, this is going to sound pretty obvious, but we have to say it: You need to be a decent writer and have some interest in it for this to be a viable online networking avenue for you. Writing is not for everyone, so don't feel you have to pursue this form of networking. But, if you do have a knack for it, consider adding this to your networking repertoire. It's also priced right in that usually no cost is associated with it at all. There's also little ongoing maintenance, because after an article you write or comment you submit goes live on the Web, your work is done.

> **Tip:** *Writing reviews of books relevant to your business or profession for Amazon (www.amazon.com) is a great way to become known. Amazon reviews tend to come up high in Google searches, so you'll enhance your digital footprint as well. Just be sure that you've actually bought and read the book you're reviewing!*

7. Online Public Speaking

Public speaking is another frequently overlooked networking method. You don't have to make a living as a full-time motivational speaker or expert lecturer to make connections and gain visibility; you can speak on an occasional basis as a way to establish your professional identity.

Public speaking online happens primarily through webinars and podcasts. If you work for an organization that uses webinars to train or convey information to employees in various locations, you are already familiar with these processes and know that they are relatively easy to use as either host or participant. If you're not familiar with webinars, you might be surprised at how much they feel like the experience of a live presentation. If you are the featured speaker for a webinar, you will upload a presentation, such as PowerPoint slides, using a Web meeting platform such as WebEx or TelSpan. You will speak about your visual presentation using traditional telephone conference calling or using Voice Over Internet Protocol (VoIP) technology, which is the routing of voice conversations over the Internet rather than through phone lines. You can encourage audience interaction through online polls or surveys and with questions texted in or asked over the voice line.

In a podcast, you are essentially broadcasting as if on the radio, but the audio feed is through computer technology instead of airwaves.

Whether you're speaking in a webinar or podcast, you'll enhance your professional stature and visibility significantly. In chapter 6, we go into more detail on how to use webinars or podcasting as an online networking tool.

Countdown to Launch

In this chapter, you've thought about what you want to accomplish in your career or business and have been introduced to the seven main ways to network online. Don't worry if you don't fully understand what some of these things are or exactly how to go about doing them. In chapters 4, 5, and 6, we provide more how-to details of using each of these online networking methods.

Key Points: Chapter 3

- Before determining which Web-based tools you'll use for networking, it's important to identify your career or business goals so that you can choose the right avenues for reaching those goals.

- Online networking is a complement to, not a replacement for, traditional "offline" networking conducted in person or by telephone.

- The seven main categories of online networking are social networks, identity-management sites, blogs, webfolios, discussion groups, online publishing, and online public speaking.

Chapter 4

Social Networking Sites: Six Degrees of Separation on Steroids

Congratulations! You've completed some of the most challenging tasks on your seven-day journey to online networking. In chapter 2, you identified the unique attributes that shape your personal brand and scripted marketing messages. In chapter 3, you defined your goals and read brief descriptions of the various choices for Internet-based networking to see which ones best fit your goals and needs.

Now, in this chapter and the two that follow, we take you beyond planning and thinking about online networking into the realm of actually doing it. Here, you learn almost everything you need to know about utilizing social networks—the benefits, features and functionalities, most popular sites, and ways to get started. You also learn some of the official and unofficial rules of engagement on these sites—the "netiquette."

In This Chapter

- Develop a deeper understanding of social networking sites and their benefits.

- Learn common features and functionalities of various social networks.

- Get started on LinkedIn.

- Identify other popular sites.

- Learn the do's and don'ts of online networking etiquette.

What Are Social Networking Sites or Services?

Social networking sites are huge online databases in which individuals upload information about themselves—usually referred to as a "profile"—for the purpose of networking with others online. In its broadest sense, the term "social networking" includes sites that have a predominantly personal focus as well as those more business and professionally oriented.

Personal networking sites focus on staying in touch with friends; making new friends; reconnecting with old contacts; sharing opinions about music, movies, and hobbies; and finding dates or romance. Sites such as MySpace, Facebook, and Classmates.com are among the most popular in this category.

Business or professional networking sites, on the other hand, focus on exchanging information for career opportunities, consulting assignments, new business ventures, job inquiries, expertise requests, business deals, business promotion, and more. Sites including LinkedIn, Ecademy, Ryze, XING, Viadeo, and an ever-expanding list of others fall into the professional networking arena.

Not to confuse matters, but these two camps are not mutually exclusive. Undoubtedly, some jobs are found and hiring done on the personal networking sites. And reconnecting with former colleagues and classmates on the business-oriented networking sites can lead to social opportunities, friendly encounters, and perhaps even dates! But the business sites vary greatly from the more personal sites in terms of information you put in your profile, search capabilities, rules of engagement, and general tone of the conversations on the sites.

This chapter focuses on the professional/business networking sites. We'll continue to use the term "social networks" because that's the proper generic term for all types of online networks that connect people, but we will always be referring to the business or professionally focused social networks. You can check out the online dating services and search for old school chums at the end of your seven-day journey!

The Benefits of Social Networking Sites

By signing up on one or more of the professional networking sites, you can dramatically increase the scope and reach of your network. Thousands or perhaps millions of other people globally can view your information 24/7! (Don't worry; you control how much personal data you put out there for people to see.) You can broadcast your message faster and farther than is possible with traditional networking and some of the other online networking options. And networking interactions are easier to schedule. You don't need to be in the same place to network. You don't even have to be networking at the same time. In other words, you can make professional connections despite time and location barriers. You can meet people on the social networking sites that you wouldn't be able to meet otherwise because of location, time constraints, physical limitations, or your level within your organization or professional community.

There are also technological benefits. You don't need to have strong computer proficiencies to use the social networking sites. Basic computer and Internet skills will suffice. So, if the thought of launching a blog or building your own personal Web site is just too daunting, the social networking sites are a good option for you. Even if you plan to start a blog or a Web site, the social networking sites should probably still be a significant part of your online strategy.

In addition, the social networking sites offer more functionality, more members, and a more diverse audience than online discussion groups (such as Google groups or Yahoo! groups). In discussion groups, a smaller number of members tend to share a similar interest and don't offer the broad range of talents and interests represented on sites such as LinkedIn and Ryze.

Why Pick Social Networking Sites for Your Online Encounters?

- They're less time and labor intensive.

- You use them on your own schedule instead of having to attend meetings or events that might not be as convenient.

- They broadcast your message faster and farther.

(continued)

(continued)

- They give access to a global audience 24/7.
- They help you unearth influential and hard-to-find people.
- You can get by with minimal computer skills.
- Everyone's doing it!

The Ever-Changing Landscape of Social Networks

Providing a comprehensive list of all the business-oriented social networking sites is a constant challenge. New sites arrive often, older ones disappear from view, and other types of Web sites expand their offerings to resemble social networks. Check out the list in the sidebar "Top Five Professional Social Networks." We're calling these "top" sites based on their popularity, membership size, and broad range of features. These sites were all functioning and going strong at the time of this writing. Several of them are so large and well established that they're not likely to dissolve any time soon.

Top Five Professional Social Networks...

- www.linkedin.com
- www.ecademy.com
- www.ryze.com
- www.viadeo.com
- www.xing.com

...and Several Up-and-Coming Ones to Watch

- www.amodus.org.uk
- www.bluechipexpert.com
- www.brightcircles.com
- www.konnects.com
- www.gobignetwork.com
- www.hooversconnect.com

- www.network2connect.com

- www.networkingforprofessionals.com

- www.zubka.com

LinkedIn, with more than 20 million members from a wide variety of backgrounds and industries, is by far the largest professional networking site and therefore gets lots of attention in this chapter. But other sites are excellent for various purposes. In fact, other large sites with diverse memberships, as well as niche sites specific to one field or industry, could be more effective and targeted for some of you. We encourage you to explore them so you can decide for yourself which one is best for you.

The various professional networking sites differ from one another in significant ways, such as headquarters location (which can affect the geographic slant of the membership), location of members, size of the membership, rules for connecting, and advanced features beyond the basic posting of a profile and browsing other people's profiles. Yet, all these sites have some common features:

- **Membership required:** You have to join the sites. Some sites are by invitation only, whereas others are open to all who find their way to the home page. But you must sign up and become a member.

- **Posting a profile:** You represent yourself on the site with a profile that you fill out. The profile provides information about your skills, work history, education, and credentials.

- **Sending and accepting invitations:** You grow your network by inviting others to join your network on the site and by accepting invitations from other people to connect to their networks.

- **Searching for contacts:** You explore the site's membership to find people. You search for people you already know but may have lost touch with. You search for people you don't know but who have something in common with you professionally or who do something or work somewhere that's of interest to you. You search by name or other criteria and reach out to the people you find to ask them to join your network. You can also request an introduction to people in their networks or start a dialogue with them to share ideas or get information and answers.

- **The Principle of six (or fewer?) degrees of separation:** All sites are based on the idea of six degrees of separation. In other words, it's not just the people you know, but the people your contacts know, and the people their contacts know, that can reap networking rewards. The premise is that if you reach out far enough (six degrees, according to the adage), you can connect to everyone. With these sophisticated technology tools and platforms facilitating the networking process, however, experts now estimate that only about four to five degrees of separation connect everyone! Regardless of the number, it is truly amazing how your network grows exponentially on these sites.

Only Three Degrees of Separation from Nearly Five Million People!

As of this writing, your author Ellen has the following network on LinkedIn:

- **1st-degree network: 924**. These are the people she has connected to directly.

- **2nd-degree network: 167,800.** These are the people her direct (1st-degree) contacts know.

- **3rd-degree network: 5,285,900.** The people in the 1st-degree networks of her 2nd-degree contacts.

- Total members she can contact directly or be introduced to: 5,454,700.

When Ellen searches her network to find contacts or assistance, she is searching a database of nearly five million people—evidence of how a network can grow exponentially when you use a social networking site.

Are You LinkedIn?

LinkedIn, a California-headquartered company, was started in 2003 and grew to more than 20 million members in just four years with no end of the rapid growth in sight. On the LinkedIn site, you find a diverse group of people—more than 150 industries represented, many countries, and all levels of people, from entry level to senior management. LinkedIn members are unemployed; self-employed; employed by small, medium, and large companies; students; and retired. All the Fortune 500 companies have members on LinkedIn, and all the Fortune 500 are represented at director level or above. There are some powerful people on this site—and a lot of regular folks, too!

LinkedIn is the clear front-runner of the professional networking sites. That's why we recommend that you start with this site and explore others later. Or, if you have time for only one site, this should be the one!

Getting Started on LinkedIn

You might have already received some invitations to join LinkedIn. If so, just accept those and that will get you started as a member. If not, go to the site (www.linkedin.com) and sign up. You don't need to have an invitation to join.

> **Tip:** *If your idea of a network is the Rolodex on your desk, think of it this way: On LinkedIn, you have not only your Rolodex, but your contacts' Rolodexes and their contacts' Rolodexes! Luckily, though, you won't need to have that huge pile of plastic on your workstation. It's all accessible on the Web.*

Perhaps you've accepted some invitations already, but, due to time constraints or lack of understanding about the site, you never got fully up and running on it. Many people fall into this category, so you're not alone. They tell us, "I think I signed up already." That might have been months or even years ago. Then someone or something triggers their desire to start working the site.

A LinkedIn Convert

A former client of ours, Doug P., recently contacted us by sending an invitation to connect to him and his network on LinkedIn. In his message he explained, "I am getting on board with the LinkedIn process. It has been a long time coming, but I am beginning to see the light!"

Obviously, he had heard one of our many LinkedIn/online networking "sermons." We're very excited and passionate about online networking, and especially LinkedIn. So we struggle to understand the drawbacks or perceived drawbacks that stop people from participating. But now, aha, we had a real live "subject" to interrogate! He was happy to respond to our questioning and provided the following explanation as to why it had taken him (a veteran salesperson, skilled networker, and active job seeker) a while to "link up" or in.

"The principal reason was (and in part still is) that I don't fully understand how to take full advantage of LinkedIn. It looked like another thing (like learning to program your iPod) that I would have to struggle through. The combination of not knowing how it works, what exactly it does for me, and

(continued)

(continued)

the time element involved with learning it (I have four small kids so not much free time) were the reasons I did not jump in right away."

He continued, "What prompted me or pushed me over the edge was an article I read in a business journal that said that more and more recruiters were using LinkedIn for reference checks and to make sure that you were who you claim to be."

Regardless of whether you are new to LinkedIn, somewhat familiar, or already to some extent on the site, now is the time to get connected, or more fully connected. Connecting is not difficult, and you don't need to understand all the details and benefits to start networking there. The steps to take for joining and enjoying a basic level of activity in LinkedIn follow.

Step 1: Set Up Your Profile

You need to set up your profile first. We recommend that you provide comprehensive profile information, so plan to spend some time on this step. Your profile helps former colleagues, clients, prospects, and potential business partners find you. You want to ensure that everyone who may know you is able to connect to you on LinkedIn.

Almost everything that is on your resume should be in your LinkedIn profile. There is no option to actually upload a resume, per se. But you can cut and paste your resume information there.

Although setting up your profile on LinkedIn is easy, you should set aside a block of time to accomplish this task. Or you can work on it in several sessions. Doing this is well worth the investment of time, so don't get impatient. Recognize that this is the critical first step.

Be Careful About What You Include

Be thoughtful and cautious about what you include in your LinkedIn profile because millions of people—including current and former bosses and colleagues—may be viewing it tomorrow!

- Be truthful and accurate. Lying is not acceptable.

- Be thorough but concise. Your profile shouldn't tell your whole life story.

● Make sure your spelling and grammar are up to par.

● If you aren't sure how you are coming across, ask some colleagues for suggestions.

The process of signing up, completing your profile, and selecting certain privacy options is easy and intuitive, but if you would like the guided-tour version, here it is.

After going to the LinkedIn Web site at www.linkedin.com, you will be asked to enter the following if you are joining for the first time:

● **Your name**

● **E-mail address:** LinkedIn allows you to enter more than one e-mail address for yourself if you think that people might send invitations to you at different addresses, such as work and personal. You do, however, have to select one address where you want messages sent to you from LinkedIn.

● **Password:** You'll be asked to create a password.

● **Country**

● **ZIP code**

● **Status:** Choices are employed, business owner, looking for work, working independently, student.

● **Industry:** You pick one from a comprehensive list.

● **Education:** Select the state, then choose an institution from a drop-down menu, and then select the dates attended.

● **Goals for LinkedIn:** Check off things you would like to accomplish on LinkedIn. There are many options, including "hear from old colleagues," "provide references for former colleagues," etc.

● **Work History:** Add your work history. If you are currently unemployed and seeking a new opportunity, you can list that as your current company: "Seeking new [insert job title or function] role." Add prior positions/titles and employers, too. Your data here will be in narrative or paragraph form (no bullets). Again, list all work history shown on your resume. This will help others find you and automate the process of extending invitations to former colleagues. We tell you more about how that works later in this chapter.

- **Websites and Blogs:** LinkedIn lets you insert links to a few other sites. These would typically be to your webfolio or blog, but can also be to sites about your books or other publications or to quotes about you in articles. They might also be to organizations that you have some affiliation with, such as professional associations you're a member of or a company you work for. Check your links periodically and update them if necessary. Be creative, but keep it relevant to your personal brand.

- **Other sections:** There are other sections that invite you to list your, **Interests** (a keyword list separated by commas), **Affiliations**, and **Honors and Awards**.

- **Summary:** This is the place where you'll enter your self-marketing sound bite (developed in chapter 2). You might also have a profile or summary section at the beginning of your resume that you can use here. This section should provide readers with an overview of your skills and experience (your positioning statement or personal brand) and any networking objectives.

> **Tip:** *Don't overlook the section called Public Profile. This is your unique Uniform Resource Locator (URL) that will take visitors directly to your page on LinkedIn. As you are signing up, it will appear as www.linkedin.com/in/ followed by combinations of numbers and letters. Be sure to change the last part to your name. This gives you additional online presence and will further your name recognition on Web searches.*

- **Specialties:** This affords you a place to list your keywords. You may already have a section called "Keywords" on your resume. They might include job titles, industry names, product names, acronyms known in your field, software programs related to your work, specific skills that set you apart from others—any words that someone doing a keyword search might use to find you. Be sure to use all variations of your keywords—full names, abbreviations, acronyms—to increase the chance that you will be found in searches.

To keep track of your progress as you work on your profile, you can view the LinkedIn status bar, which shows visually and by percentages how complete your profile is. Of course, your goal is to get to 100 percent, but you can always go back and add to or edit your profile later. For now, aim to make it thorough enough to present you favorably, knowing that you can enhance it in the future. You might also have to come to terms with never reaching 100 percent because for example, in order to do so, you must include a photo of yourself and you might not want to post your photo.

No matter what you choose to include in your profile, LinkedIn lets you select how much of your profile data you want to make public, as you can see in figure 4.1.

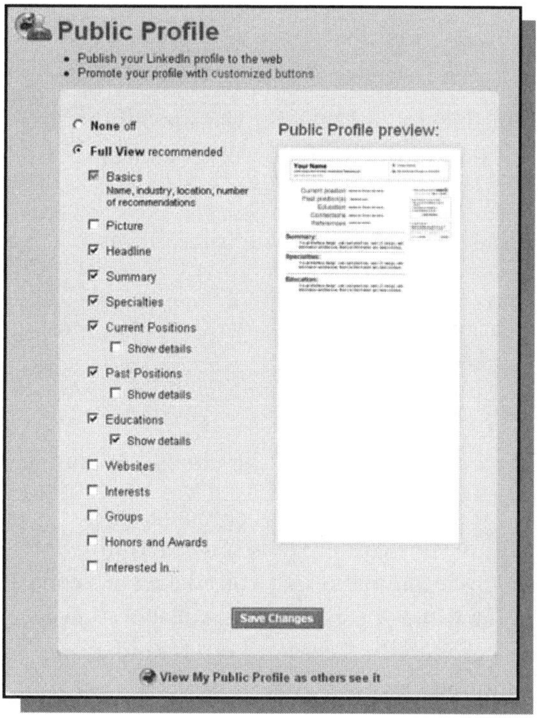

Figure 4.1: LinkedIn allows you to choose which portions of your profile you make public.

Step 2: Customize Your Membership Using the Accounts and Settings Tab

After setting up your profile, click on the Accounts and Settings tab, where you select the type of membership you want and can customize how you want your membership to function.

The first thing you'll do in the Account and Settings section of the site is to choose your level of service by selecting either the free version of LinkedIn or one of the fee-based options. We have both put our monies where our mouths are and opted to upgrade our accounts to versions with more features and more ways to connect with people. The cost of most of these premium plans is modest and affordable.

The free version is very robust, though. You can do what you need to do, at least initially, with the free service. So you might want to try the free option for a while before electing to upgrade.

Settings gives you lots of options or forces you to make a number of decisions—whichever way you choose to think about it! You can do the following:

- **Upload a photo.** When this feature of LinkedIn was introduced in late 2007, it caused a great deal of discussion on blogs and LinkedIn forums. Opinions ran the gamut:

  > "Feels too much like the personal networking sites, seems unprofessional."

  > "Will create discrimination issues, especially with so much hiring happening through LinkedIn."

  > "Helps to be able to put a face with a name!"

  You aren't required to post a picture. And you can choose, in another section, whether to view others' photos.

- **Choose to allow or not allow your connections to view your own connections list.** We strongly recommend that you make your connections visible to others. That type of sharing and collaboration is the point of participating in LinkedIn. People who refuse to share their contacts risk being snubbed by other members.

- **Choose to notify your network when you make significant changes to your profile.** You will ultimately want people to be notified when you earn a promotion, complete a degree or certification, or launch a new business. While you are frequently tweaking your initial profile, however, we recommend turning off this feature because you don't need your contacts to be notified every time you make a change to it.

There are some other choices to make in this section as well. You can indicate how you wish to receive invitations, messages, notifications, and introductions, or you can simply elect the default settings until you get a feel for the site.

Rest assured that there is a great deal of privacy and protection built into the LinkedIn process. LinkedIn is not the typical contact-management tool that allows you to collect and store phone numbers, addresses, and other data about your contacts. No one can change your information except you. No one can connect to you without your permission. And if you want to disconnect from someone, you can do that easily and with no notice generated to them saying that you dropped them from your network.

Once you've completed your profile and chosen your account settings, you are ready to grow your network on LinkedIn.

Step 3: Invite Others to Join Your Network

Now that you have completed your LinkedIn profile, you need to connect with others. People you know might already be on LinkedIn, but you are not connected to them until one of you sends an invitation and you accept that invitation.

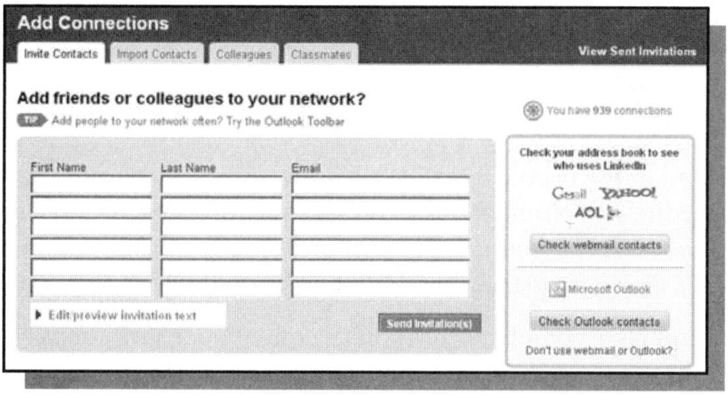

Figure 4.2: LinkedIn makes it easy to invite new contacts, existing contacts, or former colleagues and classmates to join your network.

From the home page, click on Add Connections on the left side of the site. From the next screen (an example of which is shown in figure 4.2), you'll see four options for issuing invitations:

1. Simply key in the first name, last name, and e-mail address in the grid at the center of the screen. You can enter up to six names and e-mail addresses and invite them all simultaneously.

2. Import your contacts (if you have contacts stored in Outlook, Gmail, AOL, or Yahoo!) and simply check off those you would like to invite.

3. Click on the Colleagues tab at the top of the screen. LinkedIn automatically searches its entire member database to find all persons who indicate that they work or worked for any of the organizations listed in your profile. For each employer, you can view a list of names and titles (a long list, likely, if you have worked for large organizations) and check those you'd like to invite.

> **Tip:** *The LinkedIn feature that identifies past and present colleagues to facilitate sending invitations is one of the key reasons to include all your work history in your profile. If you omit any of your past employers from your work history list, LinkedIn has no way to reconnect you with people you may have worked with there.*

4. Click on the Classmates tab at the top of the screen. LinkedIn automatically searches for members who attended your alma maters during the years you attended. Simply check those you'd like to invite.

With options 3 and 4, the people receiving your invitations are already members of LinkedIn. In options 1 and 2, they may or may not already be on the site. To those persons, you may want to include a brief explanation about LinkedIn in your invitation in case they aren't familiar with the site.

In any case, we strongly recommend that you customize your invitations instead of using the standard LinkedIn invitation that says

> "I'd like to add you to my professional network on LinkedIn."

Sending that canned note is a sure sign that you didn't take the time or care enough to personalize the invitation to remind the invitees who you are and how they know you. Such a message may even be viewed as "spam" by some seasoned LinkedIn members.

We've seen some terrible invitations and some great ones. Following are some of our favorites (good ones).

Clearly an experienced and enthusiastic online networker!

> Hi,
>
> I found your interesting profile in my network, but we are not directly connected. If you want to connect, feel free to send me an

invitation. Or let me know if you run out of them, and I will send you one.

I was also thinking that, if you are not already a member, you should consider [suggests another site]. It could be an ideal resource for you. Membership is free and takes only minutes to register. One signal of the exclusivity and caliber of the people and opportunities is the fact that [other site name] is by invitation only. You can enter through [gives link to Web site]. If you have further questions, do not hesitate to ask me.

Have a great day!

A clever approach, yet a nice brief message.

I saw your profile on LinkedIn. You are someone that I would like to know. Hopefully you will connect with me, and I look forward to the opportunity build our networks.

Thanks.

Flattery is always appreciated!

Hi,

I am a former student and lecturer at [college name/alma mater shared by the recipient of this invitation]. I received my MA in 2000 and recognize you as a leader in the field of education. I would be honored for you to join my growing list of contacts.

Regards,

Short and sweet.

I came across your profile and would like to invite you to join my professional network on LinkedIn.com.

I trust that our connection will lead to a beneficial relationship for us in the future.

A nice friendly tone plus a little networking philosophy.

I have found that the only way to build real networks and networking opportunities with others is to take an active approach by contacting those whom I feel could benefit by networking with me. LinkedIn is the perfect online community for people to connect with each other and build diverse networks.

I would like to add you to my professional network on LinkedIn and create an online relationship where we can work together and help each other.

Please accept my invitation.

Your new LinkedIn friend!

Outlines what you can expect from this connection.

I think you might be open to adding new connections. I would appreciate if you could join my network.

I forward messages for LinkedIn members quickly and help members when time allows. I believe giving is receiving, and that helping others is helping myself. My network is one of the largest and a proven reliable route for members. By joining my network, you can also expand your network and find more business/professional opportunities.

Looking forward to networking with you. Thank you for your time and best wishes.

An active networker.

Are you open to adding connections?

Unfortunately, I reached the maximum number of invitations allowed by LinkedIn. So should you consider contacts beneficial, please do not hesitate to go to my LinkedIn profile [provides his LinkedIn URL] and send your invitation to [name and e-mail address].

This last person mentions that he has exhausted his supply of invitations. You have a lifetime limit of 3,000 invitations that you can send on LinkedIn. That's probably more than enough for most of us. But some of the active open networkers on the site do run out. LinkedIn has been known to issue additional invitations in increments of 500. But just in case, you should not be indiscriminate in handing out invitations.

Don't Get Your Account Frozen

Although you do want to develop a large network, it's important to issue invitations thoughtfully and cautiously. People receiving invitations to join your network choose one of three responses: Accept, Archive, or "I Don't Know _____" (LinkedIn inserts the sender's name in the blank). If just five people select "I Don't Know _____" when you send them invitations, your account on LinkedIn is frozen. With appeals to the LinkedIn customer service department, you may be reinstated, but we recommend taking some preventive measures to avoid that problem.

- Jason Alba, accomplished networker and author of *I'm on LinkedIn—Now What?* suggests that you ask people outside of LinkedIn (via e-mail or during traditional networking conversations) if they will join your LinkedIn network. When they say "yes," you can extend the invitation through LinkedIn and have confidence that your invitees will accept because you've given them a heads-up.

- Jim Browning, an Atlanta sales and marketing leader who offers training on LinkedIn to job seekers and networking groups, recommends that you include a statement in your invitation: "If you do not wish to connect, please do not select the 'I Don't Know Jim' button. Instead, click 'Archive.'"

Quality Versus Quantity: How Large Should You Grow Your Network?

So much has been written about the topic of growing your network. If you read any of the blogs about LinkedIn or join an e-mail discussion group about LinkedIn or other social networks, you are sure to get plenty of information on this topic.

What's all the fuss about? There are two seemingly opposite philosophies about how you should grow your network. The labels applied to these two approaches are typically "Quality" and "Quantity."

- The **quality** side is what LinkedIn as an organization advocates. On the site itself, you'll see the admonition to "Only connect to those persons that you know and trust." One of our colleagues prefers this approach. She can't imagine having little-known acquaintances in her first-level network. She accepts invitations only from people she knows well and can recommend to others.

- The **quantity** side believes that the larger the network, the better. The goal of this group is to have many contacts to increase their reach. Some LinkedIn members have more than 20,000 first-level contacts. Do they know all those people personally? Of course not! We have adopted this approach to growing our own LinkedIn networks. The larger our networks, the more apt we are to have a contact that one of our clients or other contacts might need. There's a term for this now…"promiscuous linkers," those who will connect not only to people they know well, but also to people they know marginally well, or don't know at all! Okay, so we admit it. We are promiscuous linkers!

We take exception to the quality versus quantity labels and the inference that these two approaches are mutually exclusive. We don't agree with the idea that only people you already know well can be high-quality contacts. Neither do we believe that people with large networks have somehow jeopardized the quality of their connections. Years of networking experience— our own and our clients—have produced many examples in which close contacts may provide little networking support, whereas other people, practically strangers, render invaluable assistance. Still, knowing your first-level connections well does yield some degree of confidence that they will accept your phone calls or e-mail and entertain your requests. That's a good thing.

Obviously, labels aside, there are solid arguments for both sides, which keeps the discussions going. You will probably have your own personal preference along the quantity versus quality continuum. Choose your approach based on your networking goals as well as your comfort level with the process. You can monitor the size and shape of your network on the home page by choosing Contacts and then selecting Network Statistics (see figure 4.3).

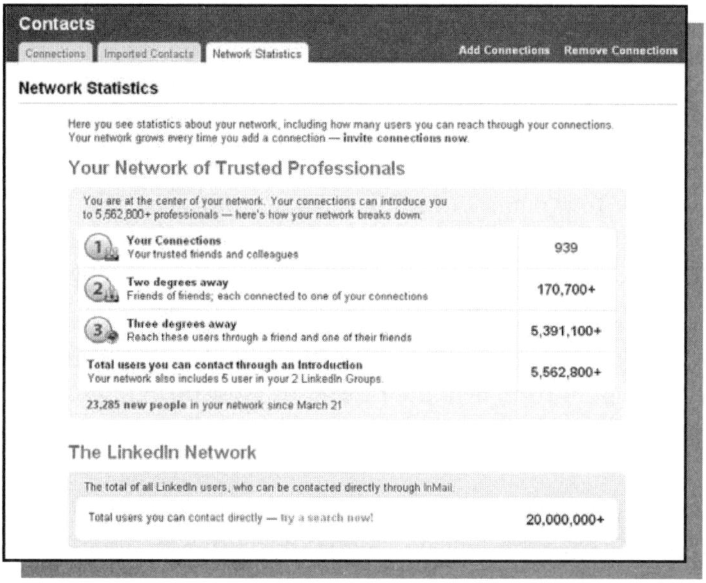

Figure 4.3: LinkedIn helps you keep tabs on the size and scope of your network.

Seeking and Offering Endorsements

With your network growing (at a rapid rate, we hope), you are ready to add some endorsements. "Endorsement" is LinkedIn's term for a reference or recommendation. Colleagues, bosses, vendors, customers, or others can write an endorsement of your work (in connection with one of your positions listed in your profile). You then approve that endorsement and make it public on your site…or not, as you wish. You can't, of course, edit what your references write, but you can try asking them to make changes if their endorsements contain errors or aren't to your liking. The process is much like the way you would coach a boss on providing a letter of recommendation or verbal reference offline.

Some people will volunteer to write an endorsement for you or will even surprise you by sending an endorsement without your having to ask. If you are in job search mode or customer acquisition mode, asking people for an endorsement on LinkedIn is perfectly fine. Typically, this would happen as you are finalizing the more traditional offline list of references.

The caveat to this approach is that endorsers need to be members of LinkedIn. They don't need to have complete profiles and be active users; just basic profile information and a free membership level will enable them to write an endorsement for you.

Don't forget that you can also write an endorsement for your references and service providers. Your name and a link to your profile page will then show up on their profile. And writing an endorsement often yields a reciprocal endorsement. Most importantly, it's a nice way to help someone.

If your references or people you would like to endorse haven't heard about LinkedIn or joined, you can share information about the site and online networking, which can, in turn, help their career or assist them in growing their business. After all, networking online and offline is all about giving back, sharing information, and helping others.

Endorsements need to be genuine. Some people, in attempting to maximize their number of endorsements, misuse this feature by requesting references from people they just met at a networking event. Don't do that. Ask only true references—former bosses, colleagues, customers, and vendors. And if you are approached to write a reference for someone you don't know well or prefer not to endorse, find a diplomatic way to say "no."

Endorsements are great. Someone is willing to say nice things about you to the vast LinkedIn world! Having endorsements is very impressive to recruiters and prospective customers and can even make the reference-checking process easier and quicker.

Searching for Jobs

LinkedIn has become a popular place to promote and peruse positions online. In fact, those in the know estimate that approximately half of the activity on LinkedIn is related to job search.

Recruiters and employers are choosing to advertise positions there. The cost is reasonable, considering that the LinkedIn audience is very large. And LinkedIn, as we mentioned in chapter 1, is a place where employers and recruiters can find passive candidates (those not specifically looking for new positions) as well as active job seekers.

Candidates are choosing to look for new positions on LinkedIn. Many positions are advertised on LinkedIn, which offers a robust search engine to find them. LinkedIn is also now an aggregator site, meaning that it pulls positions that match your criteria from other sites, including Monster,

CareerBuilder, Yahoo! HotJobs, and craigslist. Not having to visit a number of sites individually can be a major timesaver for busy job hunters.

The search engine is similar to those on the major job boards. You can search for positions by keyword, title, function, industry, company, location, level, and date of job posting (see figure 4.4).

And there is one more benefit to searching for jobs on LinkedIn. LinkedIn provides a free software tool called "Jobs Insider." You download this tool to your computer. Then, when you find a posted opportunity, the software will alert you if you have LinkedIn contacts in that organization. This enables you to use your LinkedIn network to secure an introduction to the organization and to help get your resume noticed.

Even if you aren't in job search mode, you can still benefit from this section of LinkedIn by doing competitive research. Seeing the staffing activities of your competitors can provide much information about their strategies and growth.

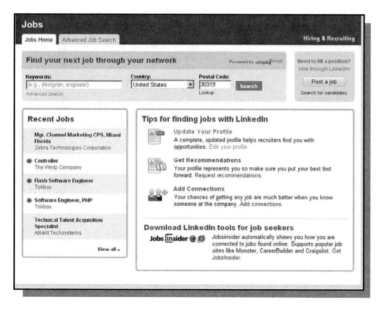

Figure 4.4: Searching for jobs posted on LinkedIn or on other Web sites is easy.

Searching for Contacts

One of the primary reasons to be on LinkedIn is to have access to a wide network of contacts when you need them. Keep in mind that when you search for contacts, you are searching your first-, second-, and third-level contacts. The more contacts you have, and the better connected those contacts are, the larger the database of LinkedIn members you'll be searching.

You can search for people by name, keyword, company (current or prior), title (current or prior), location, or industry (see figure 4.5). The search engine is powerful, allowing more complex searches using "and" and "or" and multiple search criteria.

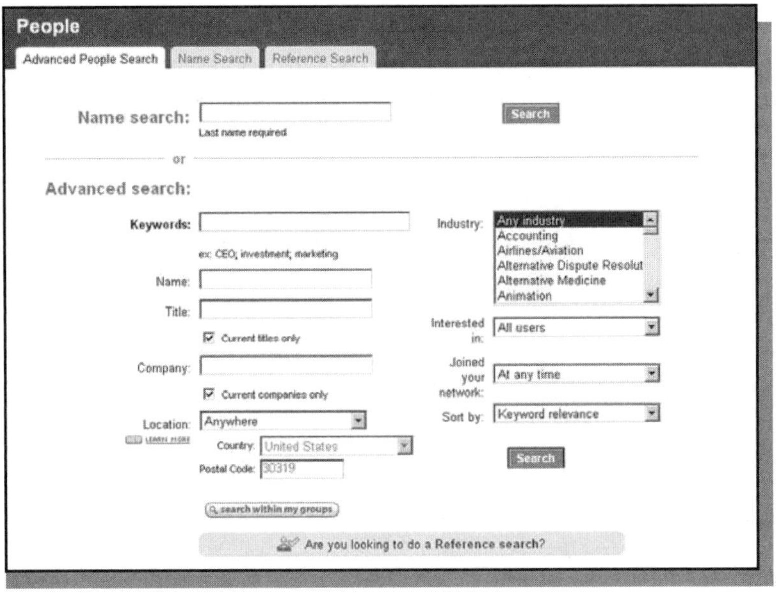

Figure 4.5: The Advanced Search screen allows you to fine-tune your search for precise results.

You can also sort your search results by keyword relevance, degrees away from you, educational degrees, number of recommendations, or number of connections.

You'll notice three columns on the right side of the search results page with numbers in them. For each individual on the list of matches for your search, these columns show—from left to right—the level of connection (1, 2, or 3 degrees away from you), their number of endorsements, and, finally, their total number of first-level connections. Their number of connections on LinkedIn can be very useful. If you have multiple people to approach (many people come up as a match when you do a search), you might want to approach first the people with the most connections. Someone with only a few contacts in LinkedIn might be less invested in the LinkedIn process and less likely to respond to an invitation or request for introduction.

Getting in Touch with Contacts

Let's say that you've just completed a search for people (see the preceding section), and you've flagged a number of individuals. What do you do now? How do you contact them?

If a contact is in your first-level network, you will be able to see that person's e-mail address in his or her LinkedIn profile and can make contact directly by sending a regular e-mail outside LinkedIn.

If a contact is a second- or third-level connection, you will probably not have the person's e-mail address (unless that person has provided it in his or her "name" field or elsewhere in the profile—the sign of an "open networker"). With no e-mail address to contact that person directly, you can select one of two buttons at the bottom of his or her profile page: either Get Introduced or Contact Directly.

Selecting Get Introduced brings up a screen on which you will create two e-mail messages: one to the person you are ultimately trying to reach and the other to the person who is your immediate contact and will be passing along your request for an introduction.

Selecting Contact Directly gives you the option to send an Inmail, an e-mail–like communication that is sent to the person through LinkedIn. This option circumvents the chain of introductions required to "Get Introduced." Depending on specific benefits of the membership plan you select, you may get a few to several free inmails. But once you use up your allotment, with the free LinkedIn service, you have to pay for each Inmail.

Both methods of contacting LinkedIn members have some pros and cons. Being introduced through the chain of contacts is more of a warm lead, a request presumably coming to them from others they know who have passed it along. On the other hand, there is always a chance that someone in the chain of two or three people may not forward it on, or at least not in a timely manner.

Sending an Inmail gets respect. People know that you have paid money to reach out to them, either a fee for that Inmail or by having paid fees for upgraded services. But it's still a cold contact—someone you are only indirectly connected to.

If you have time for the chain of communications, we recommend starting with the introduction approach. If you need to reach someone quickly or the introduction process isn't working, try sending an Inmail.

The Three I's of Initiating Contact

Our favorite LinkedIn trainer, Jim Browning, attempts to clarify the three I's of connecting to people on LinkedIn, an area that often creates confusion for people new to LinkedIn.

- **Invitation:** Inviting others to join your network or accepting their invitation. When an invitation is accepted, you will be in each others' first-level contacts. This is free. LinkedIn allots 3,000 invitations to each member, and invitations sent to you by others do not count against that total. There is no cost to issue or accept invitations.

- **Introduction:** Asking that your contacts introduce you to one of their first- or second-level contacts. The chain of communication goes from you, to your contact, to the target contact, or to another intermediary contact, and then to the target contact. These are also free, and, with the free LinkedIn account, you have five of these to use at any time. You are credited back when the introductions are or aren't forwarded, restoring you to five available.

- **Inmail:** Sending an e-mail-like communication directly to someone not in your first-level network through the LinkedIn communication channel. With the free LinkedIn account, there is currently a $10 charge for each Inmail. A varying number of Inmails are included with the upgraded memberships.

Posting Questions

One of the more recent features on LinkedIn is the opportunity to post a question to the network. You can ask questions to your immediate network or to the entire LinkedIn database.

This is a wonderful feature! Imagine that you need help with a software application, advice on the best blogging platform, or recommendations of suppliers. Here is a ready network of millions of people, some of whom have undoubtedly been in your position with the same questions or concerns. Throw the question out there and see how quickly you begin to accumulate some great advice. We've tried this feature and had useful responses within seconds of posting our question.

A few people misuse this question feature as an unsubtle advertising message for their business or services, or just for shameless self-promotion. "Do you have a need for a...?" This is not considered to be good LinkedIn form and will usually be highlighted as spam to the LinkedIn team. Don't do it. It is certain to create more ill will than goodwill.

Know the Rules!

It's a good idea to actually read the LinkedIn User Agreement. We know, user agreements can be boring. But the LinkedIn User Agreement outlines important rules for interaction and provides a code of conduct. Knowing and playing by the rules can keep you on good terms with other members and the LinkedIn team.

Other Professional Networking Sites

LinkedIn has become a favorite of most online networkers. But, as mentioned earlier in this chapter, it's by no means the only professional networking site. Following is brief information to help you select alternative or additional sites for your professional networking.

XING

Now headquartered in Hamburg, Germany, this site was previously known as Swiss-based Open BC. XING has more than five million members and is truly a global site (now boasting a multilingual platform in 16 languages). It appears to be especially strong in Europe and Asia, but many of our U.S. contacts are enthusiastic members.

Ecademy

Headquartered in the UK, this site is a social network for businesspeople worldwide. It has a strong entrepreneurial focus and less of a job search focus. Ecademy combines online interaction with offline networking events in major cities. It boasts 300,000 members globally.

Ryze

Ryze was founded in California by a technology executive and investor. The name is derived from people helping each other rise up through quality networking. It now has 500,000 members in more than 200 countries. The site hosts special networks for organizations to help members interact with each other, as well as offline meetings in many major cities.

Viadeo

Founded in France in 2003, this was initially a private networking venue. Now it's a public site for business networking, with over two million members and 3,000 joining each day. It's international in scope, with users networking in seven languages and more to be added soon. Viadeo allows searches out four levels (compared to LinkedIn's three levels).

Facebook

You may be surprised to see this site included in our list of top professional networking sites. It began as a purely social networking site for college students but is increasingly used by professionals for business networking. Because of its purely social roots, Facebook makes it easy to communicate with other members. Its size and popularity—67 million active users—convinced us to add it to this top list. Facebook is headquartered in California.

Do's and Don'ts on Social Networking Sites

Whether you are networking on LinkedIn, XING, Viadeo, or other sites, the written and unwritten rules of behavior are much the same. Here are some tips to help you get the most from your networking activities and to keep you in the good graces of other members.

Do's

- **Create a complete profile on each site.** Make yourself appealing online. Make sure that your professional image on these business networking sites isn't tarnished by radically different portrayals of your personality on some of the personal networking sites. Consistency in your profile, site to site, is also important, so ensure the same level of detail and quality regardless of the site it's on. If you can't keep your profile up-to-date on multiple sites, it's better to stick with just one site (or just one personal and one professional).

- **Grow your network.** Whether you subscribe to the "bigger is better" theory or are more comfortable with the "close and personal" strategies for growing your network, you need a reasonable number of connections to make good things happen. How you define "reasonable" depends on your field and your needs, but for many people, a reasonable size of online network might be at least 50 to 150 people.

- **Facilitate introductions.** As part of a large online network, you should help other people connect. You can recommend them if you know them and are comfortable doing so. Or just say, "for your consideration" if you don't know them well. The old theory about "my reputation is on the line" when making introductions is, in our opinion, just that—old!

- **Remember your manners.** Treat people virtually as you would in face-to-face gatherings—kindly and with respect. Don't wear out your welcome or bombard them with repeated requests for introductions to others. They are likely to drop you from their networks.

Don'ts

- **Be selfish.** Remember that networking is a two-way street. You need to give as well as you get, help other people, and not just be looking selfishly at how you can benefit from the interaction.

- **Have unrealistic expectations.** Don't expect something good from every connection. Just as in live networking settings, not every contact is a helpful contact. But even if you don't see yourself doing business with someone, you never know whom that person might know or how you might provide assistance to him or her or one of that person's contacts in the future.

- **Try to accomplish too much too fast.** Build rapport first. Just as you wouldn't walk up to someone at an initial meeting and immediately ask for favors, introductions, jobs, or business deals, you shouldn't do that online, either. Wait until the person knows you and has some investment in helping you connect, likely in a second or third conversation or exchange.

- **Spend all your time online and ignore offline networking strategies.**
Both are important, and the need to meet people face-to-face or by
phone will be a constant in our business and professional lives.

The Future of Social Networking

Certainly, social networking sites with a business or professional orienta-
tion are here to stay. Every site we've joined and profiled here is growing at
a rapid rate as more and more people become aware of the many benefits
of networking through this medium. Having 24/7 networking capabilities,
access to contacts globally, and essentially the world at your fingertips is a
big draw to everyone. In addition, introverted people love being able to
network at their computers instead of facing the crowds at traditional networking events.

The sites themselves will continue to evolve. New sites are being started all
the time. Some don't make it and disappear from view. Some start out as
other types of sites and then add features that move them into the social
networking arena. And there will also be ongoing crossover between the
personal networking sites and the professional networking sites. (Facebook
is a good example of this movement.)

Some Sites to Keep an Eye On

Plaxo began as a personal online contact manager and calendar (kind of an
Internet-based address book). Spoke describes itself as the largest online
directory of businesspeople. But both appear to be venturing into social networking territory, offering more features to find and connect with people,
not just store contact information.

HooversConnect is the latest entry into the professional social networking
arena. It was introduced in late 2007 by Hoovers and Visible Path, companies with advanced technology and vast business information resources at
their disposal. With this level of corporate sponsorship, HooversConnect is a
site to watch—and join!

Mashable.com isn't a social networking site. Rather, it's a popular blog on
social networking. Blogger Pete Cashmore, a new-media expert, writes
about various social networking sites and trends, providing an "extensive
and useful resource" and ongoing insight into the ever-changing world
of social networking.

Professional networking sites are still a relatively new concept. Even the largest and most established sites are only a few years old. So don't get too attached to any one site. Other options will certainly develop in the coming months and years.

Key Points: Chapter 4

- Social networking sites are large databases in which individuals upload information about themselves for the purpose of networking with others online.

- The term *social networking sites* includes those that have a predominantly personal focus as well as more business and professionally oriented sites. This book focuses on the professional networking sites.

- Social networking sites provide access to a global audience 24/7.

- Popular professional sites include LinkedIn, Ecademy, Ryze, Viadeo, and XING, among others.

- On LinkedIn, the largest of the sites, individuals can upload their profiles, build networks of contacts on the site, search for contacts, seek and offer endorsements, look for jobs, post questions, and advertise business services.

- Rules of accepted behavior on social networking sites dictate that you treat others with respect, focus on building rapport as you would in face-to-face networking, and facilitate introductions for others.

- The social networking landscape is changing rapidly. New sites are starting all the time, and other types of sites are migrating into the professional networking arena.

Chapter 5

Blasting Your Way Through the Blogosphere

In chapter 3 you learned a bit about blogging, both having your own and commenting on other people's blogs. Not sure it's right for you? Neither was Dan Greenfield, a new-media expert and former vice president of EarthLink. "I was reluctant at first to blog," Dan told us, "unsure if I had enough to say and afraid I would say the wrong thing, but deciding to blog was one of the best decisions that I have ever made professionally. I strongly encourage others to blog. My blog has been invaluable, giving me insights into my profession, helping me make contacts, and leading to speaking opportunities."

We'd like you to reap similar rewards by following the advice offered in this chapter. We'll help you start your own blog or learn how to say the right things on other blogs.

In This Chapter

- Decide whether blogging is a good option for you.
- Learn to speak the language of blogging like a native.
- Comment on others' blogs without putting your foot in your mouth.
- Start your own blog in a few easy steps.

Back to the Basics of Blogging

If you're new to blogging, the process and technology might seem somewhat mystifying. In fact, blogs are quite simple. A blog is really just a Web site like any other Web site, except that the content is more dynamic and interactive. All blogging software is designed to support this interactive nature, and it is easy to add and change content in a blog. You don't necessarily need to be a technology buff or expert in HTML coding.

Blogs Are Dynamic

Unlike a traditional Web site, in which content is written and uploaded to the site and then essentially just sits there until updates are needed, a blog contains frequently updated content that makes it more like a diary or journal. That's where the word "blog" comes from; it's derived from "Web log." Content is often posted daily or a few times a week, or at least much more frequently than on most Web sites.

Blogs Are Interactive

The other factor, and perhaps the most important one, that distinguishes a blog from a regular Web site is that most blogs allow input from readers. They generate conversation. You, as the owner or author of a blog, post your thoughts on your blog that other people can read. Blogging technology then allows your readers to comment, reply, rebut, expand on, or otherwise make known their thoughts and opinions about what you've said. Blogs are therefore an excellent networking tool because they not only allow you to express your personal brand through your writing, but also build community.

Same Features but Different DNA

Blogs might sound a lot like discussion groups or online bulletin/message boards, but blogs reflect more the singular voice and brand of the person or persons who "own" the blog. The blog owner is the principal author who sets the tone for the discussion, poses the discussion topics, and manages the content of the site. Discussion groups tend to be more free-for-alls. Anyone interested in a particular topic can post questions, answers, or comments at any time. While a discussion group usually does have a moderator who might introduce a topic or approve comments before they go live on the site, that moderator is not the main voice of the group.

Wiki is software that allows ordinary people to edit a Web site quickly and easily, even when that site is not registered to them. The term "wiki" refers not only to the technology, but also to a Web site that is collaborative. Wikipedia, the amazingly comprehensive and free online encyclopedia, is one of the most widely known and largest of the wikis. Wikis differ from blogs in that they are not so much conversational as they are informational. Wikis are more like knowledge databases in which readers can share their knowledge by adding their own content to a site. Blogs, which also can be informative and informational, are more about expressing opinions and sharing experiences to start a dialogue.

So What About You? Should You Blog?

Blogging can easily be a part of just about everyone's networking efforts. If you are an entrepreneur, such as an independent consultant or freelancer, having your own blog gives you a vehicle for advertising your expertise to the world (without it looking like, or having the cost of, real advertising). If you're a job seeker, you can show off your credentials and knowledge through your posts in the hope that employers or recruiters are reading.

Commenting on other people's blogs is so easy—plus, it's free—that everyone should consider doing it. Submitting comments to blogs, particularly those that get a fair amount of traffic, can skyrocket your search engine hits, enabling you to have more of a presence online.

Regardless of your situation or particular goals, blogging can do the following:

- Increase your visibility and credibility.

- Build and reinforce your personal brand (who you are).

- Provide a mechanism for expressing yourself and reaching an audience.

- Establish yourself as a thought leader.

- Build community with other like-minded individuals.

- Demonstrate your technical acumen.

- Help you secure jobs or clients by making you more visible and prominent.

- Enlarge your personal and professional network.

- Enable you to become a published author online.

Blogging for Business Development

Louise Fletcher, founder of Blue Sky Resumes and Career Hub, finds that her blog (www.blueskyresumesblog.com) gives her direct access to clients so that she doesn't have to pay referral fees. More than 90 percent of her business comes from the Web. In addition, she has been able to establish her own voice through her blog and has built credibility as a career coaching professional.

Clearly, there are plenty of reasons to blog, so let's get started (or bump you up a notch if you've already ventured a short way into the blogosphere).

First, we define some of the lingo of blogging. Then we take you step-by-step through starting a blog or commenting on others' blogs.

The Language of Blogging Defined

When you start reading blogs, you'll run across many unfamiliar terms. Here's a quick glossary of the most important ones:

- **Archives:** Older posts stored on a blog by date that readers can access and review.

- **Blogosphere:** The term for all blogs collectively. The world of blogs. The Web-based community in which all blogs exist and are connected.

- **Blogrolls:** A listing of other blogs that are favorites of the author(s) or are being promoted for some reason. Often, these are related to the point of view or personal brand of the blog's author(s).

- **Categories:** Stored posts organized by content area. Ideally, categories serve as an "information architecture" that helps readers navigate the blog.

- **Comments:** Comments are the content that readers of a blog post to the site. Comments are what give blogs their conversational nature. They are replies to posts. Comments can show off readers' knowledge and expertise (but, of course, should do so in a humble, not boastful or self-serving way).

- **Links:** A virtual connection to another blog or Web site. Content that is hyperlinked to another site can be clicked on to take the user directly to that site, or to specific content on that site, such as an article, a post on another blog, or a bio. This is one of the big ways that the Web possesses interconnectivity and forms a blogosphere, not just isolated, standalone sites or blogs. *Note:* The link might also be to a different post within the same blog—a link to the blogger's earlier writings.

  Links are highly prized. The more links you generate, the more credibility you have in the blogosphere and the higher your level of authority.

- **Permalinks:** A permanent link to a blog post, even after the post has moved from the blog's front page and into the archives.

- **Posts:** The articles or entries that make up blogs. Posts typically reflect the distinctive voice or perspective of the author. Often editorial in tone, they can be written in a conversational or personal manner as well. Some posts contain facts and links to other sites.

- **RSS (Feeds):** Really Simple Syndication (RSS) is a Web application, otherwise known as an aggregator, that compiles specific information on the Web (summarized or in its entirety) and pushes this to a single location for ready access to the person who has subscribed to a site. It is a way to track updates to other blogs of interest without having to visit each one individually.

- **Sidebars:** The side column or columns on a blog that can contain categories, bios of the author(s), lists of services, photos, recommended books or other resources, favorite blogs (in a blogroll), and archives.

- **Tags:** The keywords associated with specific blog posts. They allow for indexing by search engines.

- **Trackbacks:** An acknowledging link a blogger uses to let another blogger know that he or she has referenced specific content. The receiving blog will typically display a list of other blogs that link to the content.

Deciding Whether You'll Start a Blog or Just Comment on Others

Think back to chapter 2's discussion of your digital footprint. Do you have negative or irrelevant digital dirt that you need to wash over? Commenting on blogs or having your own blog can give you search engine hits that help to bury the content you want to hide. Or, if you don't have much of an online presence at all, blogging is one of the best ways to have Google and other search engines come up with matches for your name.

Also, think about the goals you identified in chapter 3. How might blogging help you reach those goals?

- Are you a business owner seeking greater reach to target customers?

- Are you a subject-matter expert in your profession wanting to share your expertise, both to enhance your credibility and stature and to help others in your field?

- Are you a job seeker hoping to attract employers and recruiters so that you don't have to chase them down?

- Maybe you're a recruiter who wants to get into conversations with potential candidates to "test" them before throwing them in the ring for job opportunities.

- Or perhaps you're a happily employed person who simply wants to connect with others in your field to increase your knowledge and your network.

> **Tip:** *If your preference is to share your thoughts without inviting discussion, blogging may not be for you. A traditional Web site on which you post content but readers cannot comment, other than to send you an e-mail privately, might be the better choice for you. We discuss the how-tos of starting a Web site in chapter 6.*

Both having a blog and commenting on other blogs can help in all those situations. So the decision might come down to four key factors:

- Your writing skill and interest in writing

- A passion for your subject matter

- Time available to commit to blogging

- Level of comfort with being the focus of attention

The Writing Factor

If you're not real big on writing and don't consider it a top skill of yours, you might be better off commenting on others' blogs than having the pressure and spotlight on you as author of your own blog.

> **Tip:** *If you really want to have a blog but hate to write or don't do it very well, you can consider having a blog that consists mostly of podcasts (audio files you record) or video clips rather than written content.*

The Passion Factor

Without a genuine passion for the topics you write about, your blog is not likely to be a success. It won't be seen as useful and engaging to your readers, and it won't have longevity. Both you and your readers will grow tired of it. It might also be seen as self-serving; posting any old content without passion and true interest behind it often signals that you are using the blog only as a means of getting a job or advancing your career.

The Time Factor

Having your own blog takes more time than commenting on others' blogs. With your own, there's an expectation that you will keep it fresh and dynamic with frequent posts. Ideally, you should write daily. But regular readers typically expect that you write at least a couple or few times a week, while four to six times per month is about the minimum you can get by with. Any less and you risk losing readers.

The You Factor

If promoting your personal brand and advancing your professional agenda are paramount, having your own blog might be the best way to go. Your own blog gives you a platform for your opinions and for expressing who you are and what you have to offer. Sure, your readers are able to showcase themselves and their ideas in their comments, but it's still your show. You call the shots.

If, on the other hand, you just need to expand the reach of your network, connecting with as many people as possible, with as little time commitment as possible, to advance your career, job search, business, or other endeavor, commenting on other people's blogs or selecting another vehicle for your online networking option might be better.

It Doesn't Have to Be an Either/Or Situation

Having your own blog doesn't mean you can't also comment on other people's blogs. In fact, commenting on other blogs and including a link back to your blog will help generate more traffic for you.

Commenting on OPBs (Other People's Blogs)

Start-up entrepreneurs and seasoned businesspeople are well acquainted with the concept of OPM, or "other people's money." They borrow money from others to start a business without having to put up their own cash or to supplement their own money, or they get other people to invest money as partners in a business venture. Well, commenting on other people's blogs ("OPBs") is not all that different of a process.

Commenting on OPBs lets you establish yourself as an expert, increase your visibility, and connect with others (the online networking version of fame and fortune) without the expense and time commitment of setting up and maintaining your own blog. If you like that idea, we suggest following a few simple steps to becoming an expert OPB commenter.

Step 1: Scope Out the Blogging Landscape

Start by reading other blogs to get ideas of what seems to work and not work, and what you like and don't like, when it comes to blog content.

Don't comment just yet. Just peruse and browse. Get a feel for what is discussed and what types of comments are being made.

As you surf the Net for blogs, make note of the ones you like the most and that are most relevant to your goals or professional style and areas of expertise. These will be your "blogs of choice"—ones that you'll revisit often, subscribe to, and eventually start commenting on.

After you've reviewed a selection of blogs (over the course of minutes, hours, or days— whatever it takes for you to get a good feel for them), you should start to feel comfortable with the flow of this type of information exchange and be ready to write your own comments.

> **Tip:** To save time in identifying and keeping up with your blogs of choice, set up a Google alert at www.google. com/alerts. Google will search the Web regularly and e-mail you alerts of new blog posts that match your interests. You can also use an RSS (Really Simple Syndication) reader. Yahoo!, Google, and Bloglines. com can help you do this. With RSS, you select your preferred blogs and save them to be pulled up in a "reader" format. You can then quickly scan for updates to these blogs and choose to read part or all of a posting.

Step 2: Write a Comment

You might be chomping at the bit to write and submit a comment. How hard can it be, after all? But keep in mind that your comment on a blog becomes a permanent, archived record on that particular blog and might show up for a long time in keyword searches of your name. Because of this, take time to make sure that your comment is something you can be proud of and not cringe at if you see it come back to haunt you when your name is Googled.

Write a first draft of your comment offline and then step back and ask yourself the following questions about it:

- Am I providing useful insight and input or just saying something obvious or mundane?

- Does the comment showcase my subject matter knowledge?

- Is the comment respectful and on-topic?

- Have I used language that is understandable to the readers of this blog?

- Is the comment thought-provoking and an expression of my opinions but not so controversial that it could offend others or mar my reputation?

- Is my comment consistent with the way I would like to be perceived by people in my field or other fields?

- Does my comment support my brand—who I am, my style?

- Is my comment free of grammar or spelling errors and written in a clear, concise way?

After questioning yourself about your comment to see whether it passes muster, edit the comment as necessary and then review it one last time. You're now ready to submit it.

Step 3: Submit Your Comment

To submit your comment, go to the blog that you want to comment on and look for a navigation button labeled Comment or Post a Comment or something to that effect. (The exact wording and location of the command will vary from blog to blog.)

Click there, and you'll see a place to paste your comment. (You can also type a comment directly into the space provided, but you can easily review and edit it thoroughly offline in your word processing program and then paste it in the blog.)

After you've pasted your comment, you'll see a button to click to submit it. Reread your comment one more time to make sure nothing was messed up in the pasting; then go ahead and pull the trigger to submit!

Typical Restrictions That Might Trip You Up

Some blogs limit the length of comments. This is typically expressed in number of characters, such as "maximum 3,000 characters." So be prepared to cut out some text if you have to, although typically the space provided is ample for getting your point across in a thorough but concise manner.

You also might find that you have to register with a site or be approved by the blog owner or administrator before you can submit a comment or before your comment will go live. Just be sure to follow the rules of the blog, and you should have no trouble getting your comments published and your voice heard.

Some blogs will ask you to type in a code word or number that you see on the screen before they will post your comment. This is called word verification, and many bloggers use this tool to keep "spambots" from posting erroneous ads as comments.

In addition to, or instead of, submitting a public comment on a blog, you can also e-mail the blog author directly. E-mail addresses are not always provided on the blog site, but if they are, sending an e-mail can be a great way to let the author know that you particularly enjoyed a post and want to communicate directly about it. Or you might e-mail if you worry that your comment might be controversial, misunderstood, or taken the wrong way by the readership of the blog and want to communicate one-on-one with the author instead of posting it, to be on the safe side.

You might also e-mail the author if your comment is of a personal, private nature that you don't mind sharing with one person but would rather the whole cyberworld not see.

You can take the same approach with people who comment on the blog, in cases in which they choose to let their e-mail addresses be published below their comments. E-mailing them encourages more of a relationship-building approach to networking than the slightly more detached process of commenting publicly.

DO's and DON'Ts for Commenting on OPBs

- DO keep your facts straight and strive for accuracy if you are writing an informational type of comment.
- DO make your comments relevant to the particular posting you're responding to and to the nature of the blog in general.

- DO make your comments a clear expression of your professional identity.

- DON'T just comment on a blog as a vehicle for linking to your own blog or selling something. Make your comments genuine and useful to others.

- DON'T make inflammatory comments unless you are prepared for a backlash. Be respectful, even if you are disagreeing.

- DON'T post anything you don't want quoted, printed, or reproduced forever. Your comment will go on your permanent record!

Starting Your Own Blog

Do you prefer to be the one who starts the conversation? Do you want to showcase yourself as a leader in your field or expert on a particular topic? Having your own blog might be the answer for you. Starting one is surprisingly quick and easy, though as we've warned you before, maintaining a blog to keep it fresh and interesting does take a serious time commitment.

Follow these steps for creating a blog:

1. Choose a name for the blog.

2. Select your blog platform or host.

3. Secure a domain name (sometimes this step is part of step 2).

4. Generate content to populate your site.

5. Decide and learn how to manage comments.

6. Go live!

We walk you through the basics of each of these steps in the following sections. Keep in mind, however, that exact steps will vary depending on the blog host that you choose to use and the design and layout of your blog. Entire books are written only on blogging, so these are just the basics to help you start.

The steps outlined in this chapter are designed to get you up and running with a blog within a day or so, possibly even within minutes! Then, in chapter 7, as we take you beyond the seventh day of online networking, you'll find some more advanced tips and techniques for enriching the content of your blog and attracting readers.

Step 1: Choose a Name

Like a book, movie, football team, or newborn baby, a blog needs a name. The name you choose should convey your blog's topic focus and use terminology that will sound relevant to your target audience. It should also reflect who you are.

If creativity and innovative thinking are your hallmarks, for example, feel free to get clever with your blog's name. Dan Greenfield named his blog "Bernaise Source" (http://bernaisesource.blog.com) after Edward Bernays, considered to be the "father" of modern public relations. And, of course, there's the fun play on words with bearnaise sauce, the classic French steak sauce. Egg yolks, butter, tarragon, and shallots have nothing to do with Dan's expertise in media and PR, but the association of Bernays and bearnaise makes for a memorable blog name!

Other blog names clearly reflect the values and mission of the authors. Guy Kawasaki's "How to Change the World: A practical blog for impractical people" (http://blog.guykawasaki.com/) and "Force_of_Good: Lance Weatherby's observations of consumer technology, entrepreneurship, and more" (http://forceofgood.typepad.com/) are good examples of this.

> **Tip:** Make sure to choose names that are in the public domain and that do not include copyrighted or trademarked materials. Ask a lawyer to help if you're in doubt.

Before deciding on your own blog's name, test its uniqueness and searchability by typing it into a search engine (Google, MSN, etc.) as a keyword or keyword phrase, both with and without quotation marks around it. If nothing relevant comes up, or not many matches come up, you may have hit on a fairly unique name. You might also use your own first and last name for the blog name if they are unique enough.

Whatever name you choose, be sure to decide on it after careful consideration. Don't rush into a name you might end up not being happy with. When we decided upon CareerCandor as our blog name, for example, we brainstormed extensively and came up with a list of more than 50 names to consider. We ruled out the ones that were already taken, crossed off the ones that caused us to ask, "What were we thinking?!" and then gave careful thought to the suitability of the remaining ones before narrowing down the list to the final choice.

Step 2: Choose a Blog Platform

Your blogging software or platform is the technology that runs your blog. It's where your blog resides online. You can choose from hosted and non-hosted options. Some of these are free, whereas some come with a modest fee. We tell you more about hosted and nonhosted options later in this step, but in short, we can tell you now that most beginning bloggers choose the hosted option.

When you use a hosted service, you don't have to buy and install software or have the blog reside on your own server. Hosted services are simple vehicles for blogging, ideal for people who aren't computer gurus. Nonhosted options, on the other hand, offer more complete control over your site, more flexibility, and more design options. For example, a company would probably want to host its own site on its own server for confidentiality's sake. Or a technology expert might want to design the layout and develop his or her own site from scratch.

If you're not looking to become a professional blogger or to make a living off your blog (although you never know where your blog might lead you), a hosted service is your best bet. Nevertheless, we offer more detailed explanations of both hosted and nonhosted options next, as well as examples of both types of service providers, so that you can make your own decision about which is right for you.

Hosted Services

Hosted platforms are the easiest on both your wallet and your technical abilities. With a hosting service, you don't have to install any software. You simply access everything you need on the host's Web site. The host provides easy-to-use text editors to help you create your posts without any special technical knowledge. It also provides templates for the layout and design of your blogging site so you don't have to be a graphic artist. The process is so simple, in fact, that you can have a blog up and running in just minutes with a hosted service.

The main disadvantage of a hosted service is that you have limited control over the look and functionality of your site. Although most hosted services offer plenty of nice design templates to choose from, you are limited to the colors, graphics, and page layouts they offer. This is typically an insignificant tradeoff, however, considering the ease and cost-effectiveness of this option.

In the appendix, you'll find a complete listing of blog hosting resources, but here we've provided a quick overview of a few of the most popular ones.

- **Blogger:** Blogger is a free service that requires little to no technical expertise. You do have to use some HTML to modify some of the templates or use some of the sidebar features, but generally the service is easy to use and great for a first-time blogger.

HTML

HTML stands for Hypertext Markup Language. It's the language used to make Web content appear a certain way. When using HTML, you write in English (or any other language of your choice) as usual, but you use special coding (called "tags" or "labels") to indicate the graphic aspects of your text, such as italic or bold. Most sites requiring you to use HTML will offer a simple tutorial on it. Or you can find lots of free HTML tutorials by doing a Google search with the keywords "HTML tutorial."

- **Typepad:** Typepad requires very little to no technical expertise but does offer some fairly sophisticated options, such as a good menu of sidebar add-ons. It also has a built-in mechanism for tracking your blog's visitors, or "traffic." Typepad does have a cost, ranging from just a few dollars to double digits per month. Yearly discounts are available. With the higher priced service levels, you get more flexibility with your design template and other upgraded features. Typepad is a good choice if you are at the beginner stage now but expect to be blogging long term and want your blog service to grow with you.

- **WordPress:** WordPress is free, or you can pay a modest fee for some premium design options. WordPress is quite user-friendly but not as simple as Blogger. While your technical expertise can be minimal, it is helpful to have some tech knowledge if you want to use some of the more advanced features to move beyond beginner stage. One neat feature of WordPress is that it also offers a nonhosted option, which could come in handy if you decide to switch to a standalone blog in the future.

Nonhosted Services

Nonhosted services, also called "standalone" or "server-side" platforms, give you much more design and functionality flexibility.

To go this route, you must secure a domain name as described later in step 3. Then you'll subscribe to a hosting service and download a content management system. Note that sometimes these two steps are one and the same. The blog hosting service can often register your domain name, or if you already registered a domain name, you can go back to that same registrar and see if it offers blog hosting services. Buyer beware, though, as the registrar will try to sell you all sorts of services and packages, but that doesn't necessarily make it the best source for blogging hosting!

Is the Nonhosted Route Worthwhile?

Going the nonhosted route costs more and can tax your technical skills (or, more likely, require that you hire a Web professional to help you), but the result will be a blog with a URL in your own name on your own server that is fully customizable to your liking.

To have a standalone blog, you must use a content management platform. The most popular are WordPress and MovableType. Drupal (www.drupal.org) is also an up-and-coming option.

Can I Switch My Blog Host After Launching My Blog?

You can switch your blog platform, but not without the potential loss of some of your readership and some of your archived posts and comments. When you switch blog software, readers who have bookmarked any of your posts will lose them. So it's best to research your options thoroughly at the outset and not have to switch.

Step 3: Register Your Domain Name (Optional)

The name of your blog may or may not be the same as the domain name or URL. The URL, or Uniform Resource Locator, is basically your complete address on the Web. It's like putting street address, city, and state, plus apartment number and ZIP code on an envelope.

The domain name, on the other hand, is just the last two parts of the URL, such as "careercandor.com." The domain name is kind of like the name of an apartment building without the actual street address, city, state, and ZIP.

If you select a hosted option, using such software as Blogger, Typepad, Vox, or WordPress, you do not have to register a domain name because you'll get a domain name and URL as part of the blog hosting service. You may, however, secure a domain name anyway if you prefer.

If you decide to go the nonhosted route, you will need to register a domain name. Some popular domain registrars are www.dreamhost.com, www.networksolutions.com, www.register.com, and www.godaddy.com. On any of these sites, you can type in the name you have in mind for your blog and see if the name is available or already taken.

> **Tip:** *If you already have a Web site, you don't necessarily need to register a new domain name for your blog. Your blog can be part of your existing site. Or, if you don't have a site but have a domain name already registered, such as your own name (e.g., johndoe.com), you can use that domain name to create your blog.*

Pricing and options vary on these sites, so browse their fees and package offerings to select the one that works best for you. On many of these sites, if you pay for a year or more at a time, the service can cost less than $10 a month with no fee charged for setup of your blog. If you pay monthly, you may end up with a setup fee in the low double digits plus several dollars a month for the service. Of course, add-on options are available for premium upgrades that cost more.

Step 4: Generate Content

The needs of your audience, your goals and objectives, and your personal brand will drive your blog's content. Never lose sight of what you are trying to accomplish, whether that's a new and better job, advancement in your career at your current employer, business development and referrals, or just a sense of collegiality with your professional or business community at large. Your goals should not be blatant in your blog. Don't shove them down your readers' throats. But do make sure that the time, effort, and possibly money that you put into your blog serves to move you closer to reaching your goals. Your personal agenda, however, should not usurp your blog's ability to do some good for other people. There's no point in having a blog if it's just going to be an ego trip for you or all about getting and no giving.

Legal Implications for Bloggers

In some cases, employees are not allowed to have a blog, even if the blog's content is unrelated to the business of the employer. Blog content is a potential minefield for employees. Better to be safe than sorry, so check your organization's guidelines before jumping into the blogging fray. And don't say anything on your blog that you wouldn't want your boss, colleagues, or customers to see! Also consider a disclaimer that lets readers know that this is your personal blog and that it represents your own opinions, not necessarily those of your employer.

How to Come Up with Content

Your first few posts are easy. You have some things on your mind, so you know what to say and can easily write some posts. Maybe you even have lots of material in your files—essays, editorials, articles, or just thoughts and ideas you've written either for fun or for actual publication. In this case (assuming you have the legal right to reprint the content), you will have plenty of content to post for days, weeks, or months to come.

But what happens when the well starts to run dry? Or what if the old stuff just isn't current enough to use? That's when you need to use some of the techniques for coming up with new material. Seasoned bloggers are always on the watch for new content. Some keep a notebook to scribble ideas as they come to mind. Others seek inspiration in things they read or observe offline and online.

Whatever you do to get your ideas, it's helpful to organize content for posts and comments at least several weeks in advance to save time. On many platforms or hosted services, you can create posts for automatic publication at later dates. Of course, you can't always use stockpiled content because sometimes you'll want a post to be a reaction to current events or recent news.

Tip: *If you enjoy reading books related to your field and find yourself posting book reviews on your blog site, consider signing up with Amazon.com as an Amazon Affiliate. You can then put a graphic image of the book's cover and its title on your blog site and link the cover and title to Amazon. If your blog traffic is high and your readers buy the books you link to, you can earn some money every time someone buys the book on Amazon as a result of linking to it from your site.*

How Long Is Too Long?

Good content isn't necessarily long, so don't get bogged down writing lengthy entries to post. Good content can come in the form of a very short post, maybe even just a question to draw comments. Shorter posts consist of typically about 200 words or are even just a quick comment of a sentence or two plus perhaps a link to another site.

DO's and DON'Ts for Content on Your Blog

- DO let your unique personality and style come through.

- DO get your facts straight if you're providing information that needs to be objective and accurate.

- DO be courteous and civil toward your readers and be accessible to them.

- DO include a bio and maybe a photo (optional) so that readers can get a better sense of who you are.

- DO double-check your grammar and spelling.

- DON'T sell or pitch to readers in a heavy-handed way. And don't try to do it subtly because they'll typically see through your efforts. If you do want to promote something, be open, honest, and not pushy about it and don't do it often.

- DON'T try to be someone you're not. Be down-to-earth and genuine in your posts.

- DON'T quote from or mirror the content of other blogs excessively. Be original.

- DON'T reprint articles without asking for permission from the original source and always give appropriate attribution to the source.

Step 5: Decide How You Will Manage Comments

If blogging is all about the conversation, why is there any decision to make about the comments people want to submit to your site? Well, believe it or not, some people actually create a blog that doesn't allow comments to be posted. We don't recommend that approach because it makes your online networking one-sided.

Even if you have no qualms about allowing—even encouraging—comments, you still have the decision to make about how you will manage them. Will you allow people to publish their comments directly and immediately to the site when they click Submit, or will you serve as a moderator, reviewing the comments privately before allowing them to go live on your site?

Moderating Comments

You can act as editor for your blog by moderating and approving comments. In this way, you can keep offensive or irrelevant content or spam off your blog and publish only positive, useful, or on-topic comments. Always review and approve comments promptly, as a courtesy to your readers and to invite additional comments in the future.

If you do choose not to publish a comment, it's good form to notify the writer as to why you made that decision. It's an opportunity to educate the writer (gently and politely) about the focus and mission of your blog. Show appreciation for his or her willingness to participate in the discussion and encourage the person to write again. Of course, if a comment is highly offensive, inflammatory, insulting, or simply wacko, it doesn't deserve any response.

Responding to Comments

Just because you've approved and published a comment (or let your readers submit their own comments directly) doesn't mean your job is done until you post your next entry. Keep the dialogue going by commenting on the comment or by creating a new post that builds on the comment. This is what makes blogs truly interactive and interesting.

Step 6: Go Live!

So you've put some content on your site in the form of a first post, plus your bio, and perhaps some sidebars such as a list of services you offer if you have a business, list of favorite blogs, or maybe a book review or list of recommended books or Web sites. And you've decided how you'll manage comments. You've done all this in "practice" mode, setting up and playing around with your blog privately through your blog hosting platform before publishing it on the Web.

When you're happy with what you've done, go ahead and click the button (the exact name and location varies with the different hosts) to go live. This will make your blog visible to anyone on the Internet.

Now, you just have to watch for the comments to come in and keep posting new content!

Getting People to Your Blog

Just as you learned in chapter 2 about making yourself more visible online, you need to use similar techniques to make your blog prominent, to drive traffic to your site. This is one kind of traffic jam you actually look forward to—lots of people reading and commenting on your blog regularly.

Let all the people in your network know about your blog by e-mailing them the URL to announce the "grand opening." Also include the URL in your e-mail signature block, in your bio, and in all profiles you post on social networking sites. If you have a separate Web site, you would, of course, also link that site to your blog.

Also, be sure that your e-mail address is displayed on your blog to encourage readers to contact you directly in case they're reluctant to submit a public comment. To avoid spam, spell out your e-mail address in a way that humans will understand but "bots" (the nasty little Web "creatures" that generate spam) cannot. Example: janedoe@email.com can be written as janedoe AT email DOT com.

Search Engine Optimization and Technorati

Search engine optimization (SEO) is the process of making sure that your blog will be easily found during keyword searches on Google, MSN, Yahoo!, or other search engines. (Blogs are indexed by the major search engines.)

There are also search engines specifically for blogs. Technorati.com, for example, is the authority on what's happening on the Web, particularly when it comes to blogs. Technorati searches for and organizes blogs. It tracks the links created when bloggers link to other blogs or comment on a blog, thus identifying the most active and relevant blogs. It indexes tens of thousands of content updates every hour, so the more active your blog is and the more you have paid attention to SEO, the more "relevant" your blog will be considered.

You can use some additional techniques to increase your blog traffic or search engine optimization, including links, keywords, blogrolls, categories, and trackbacks.

Links

One way to get more play with the search engines is linking your blog to other places on the Web, such as other blogs, articles, press releases, book reviews, and more. This can also inspire other bloggers and sites to reciprocate by linking to your blog.

Also link to your own Web entries, both within your blog site and elsewhere. You can link from your main blog page to your bio page, to your profile on social networking sites, and to sites of organizations you work with or for. This creates the interconnectivity that's critical to getting more visibility and meeting more people.

Keywords

Within your blog content, keywords play a critical role in search engine optimization. There are arguments on both sides of the fence regarding keywords. Some bloggers write with SEO clearly in mind to maximize their search engine "hits," whereas others write as they normally would, assuming that they are generating keywords without really trying, sort of by default. Either way, it's important to note that keywords do play a primary role in increasing traffic. In addition to keywords in your posts, having them in your post titles and category headings can increase search engine "hits."

There is not one magic list of keywords, nor is there any set of keywords that would be right for everyone's goals and focus. Keywords are simply commonsense terms that are closely connected to your field and the topics you are writing about. They might be hot buzzwords of the moment, long-standing technical terms, or just the everyday language of your business or profession.

Blogroll

A blogroll is a listing of blogs that you include as a sidebar on your own blog site. These blogs might be your top 10 favorite sites across many topics and categories. You might like them for their content, writing style, opinions expressed, or layout and design. Or they might be ones that are particularly useful as resources to supplement information you provide and topics you discuss in your posts. They can also be blogs of colleagues, vendors, suppliers, or other people you want to support and promote. Just make sure they are likely to be useful and relevant to your readers and in sync with your personal brand.

If you say something complimentary about or link to another blog or blog post, the author of that blog might reciprocate by linking to you in his or her own blogroll, thus creating inbound and outbound links. These links help your SEO by increasing opportunities for hits when search engines crawl the Web for content. The more places your blog is mentioned on other people's blogs, the more likely it is to come up as a match.

Categories

Categories are the "road map" to your blog—the navigation tool for your readers. By organizing your posts and other content into categories, you make it easy for readers to find information on your blog site, especially older entries. An optimum number of categories is four to six, but feel free to have fewer or more depending on the complexity of your blog and how long it's been around. Too many categories can give the appearance of trying to be a "Jack of all trades, master of none."

Categories help with search engine optimization because they act as keywords. Search engines love keywords, whether they are found in a blogroll, blog posts, or category names. So your category names are just one more way for your blog to be found.

Trackbacks

WordPress, Movable Type, and other platforms include the option to have trackbacks on your blog. These are a mechanism for multiple blog sites to communicate with each other. If a blogger writes an entry on a blog that refers to an entry found on your blog, the blogger making the post or comment can notify you with a trackback "ping." This allows you to see what's being said about your blog, or specific content on your blog out in the blogosphere, and can start a discussion across several blogs rather than just between authors and readers within one blog. Instructions for setting up trackbacks will be provided in the platform or host you choose to use.

> **Tip:** *Networking is about building relationships and helping others, not simply helping yourself with a job or business opportunity. Similarly, blogging is about building relationships and sharing your knowledge and ideas with others by discussing subjects you are truly passionate about; it's not just about furthering your career. Ultimately, it's all about the conversations, not just you and your needs.*

What Lies Ahead?

Blogging is rapidly growing in popularity and shows no signs of stopping. Technorati has tracked more than 112 million blogs, with new ones being created every day. Future trends for blogging include more podcasting (audio files broadcast via the Web) and vlogs (video blogs), both of which can keep readers more engaged in your blog. Audio Acrobat and YouTube are host media worth exploring as options for adding audio and video to your blog.

You might choose not to have your own blog. You might not regularly comment on other people's blogs or in any way join in on the blogging conversation for now. Nevertheless, you need to be aware of this powerful publishing medium and ready source of information. It's an immediate and interactive dialogue that can keep you informed about topics and trends. It's an exciting movement and application of technology that is shaping and will continue to shape the future of personal, professional, and organizational communications and interconnectivity. We hope you'll at least give blogging a try to see how it may enhance your online networking efforts.

Key Points: Chapter 5

- Blogging is an interactive way to connect with people online and build your visibility and credibility.

- Deciding whether to start your own blog or just comment on other people's blogs is often based on your writing ability, passion for your subject matter, time available, and comfort level with being in the spotlight.

- To start a blog, you first should research other blogs, choose a name and platform (hosted or nonhosted), and generate content on subject matter that you have knowledge and interest in.

- Maintaining your blog involves regular posting of content, responding to comments promptly, and growing your readership.

- Drive traffic to your blog through such search engine optimization (SEO) techniques as having relevant keywords, a blogroll, inbound and outbound links, and interesting posts.

Chapter 6

Beyond LinkedIn and Blogs: More Ways to Connect Online

In the preceding two chapters, we discussed the how-tos of using business-oriented social networks and blogs to enhance your visibility and meet more people. Because blogging and social networks are likely to be the primary ways you'll network online, those methods warranted their own chapters. The remaining online networking technologies are grouped together in this chapter.

In This Chapter

- Gain a deeper understanding of how the "other" online networking technologies work.

- Learn how to use identity-management sites, webfolios, discussion groups, publishing, and public speaking to round out your online networking strategy.

Here, you'll find descriptions that build on the brief introductions in chapter 3 for identity-management sites, webfolios, discussion groups, online publishing, and Internet-based public speaking. You'll also learn more about how to get started today using these online networking avenues—or how to step up your efforts if you've already dabbled in them.

Identity-Management Sites

You already know from chapter 3 that identity-management sites such as Naymz and Ziggs are excellent ways to start developing, or improve the relevance of, your online presence. These sites help you take control of your digital footprint by allowing you to create and post a profile that gives accurate, up-to-date information about your experience, current professional activities, and goals or interests.

These services offer an interesting array of features, such as e-mail alerts when your profile is viewed and the ability to connect with other people in the network via e-mail, instant messaging, or live chats.

There is little to no downside to joining sites such as Naymz and Ziggs, so we recommend that everyone do so. If you're not already on them, how about joining right now? Both Naymz and Ziggs are excellent sites with similar features, so we recommend joining both. You can spend some time on each and then see whether you prefer to cancel one membership (which is easy to do) and focus on the other site. For demonstration purposes, we walk you through the steps of joining Naymz only, but the process for joining Ziggs is comparable.

You can join both Naymz and Ziggs in a matter of minutes. You might not be able to develop a fully fleshed-out profile or take advantage of all the features of the services, but you can at least put in your basic information and then come back later to further develop your presence on these sites.

Naymz

Go to www.naymz.com, where you'll see an option on the home page to take a tour of the site and learn the steps that are required or optional for membership. Or you can simply browse some of the sample profiles featured with links on the home page. Be sure to take one or both of these steps before joining so that you get a feel for how profiles sound before you enter your own.

Step 1: Join

After becoming familiar with the site and what type of content people include in their spaces on it, you're ready to join. You'll see spaces on the home page where you enter your first and last names, e-mail address, and a password that you create. Fill in this information and click Join.

Step 2 (Optional): Import Contacts

You then have a choice of importing your contacts from several places where you might happen to keep listings of people you know, including LinkedIn, Yahoo! Mail, MSN, AOL, Gmail, Hotmail, and .Mac. Importing contacts is safe because Naymz will not get in touch with these people unless you request that it send an invitation to them. It will not publish or share your list with others, either. If you prefer to skip this step, however, you may do so. You can always come back to it later.

Rating Your Reputation

To differentiate itself from the many other sites where you can post a profile, Naymz allows you to earn what it calls "RepScores." When you have RepScores, visitors to your profile can be more confident that they are getting to know a reputable professional. The scores also open doors for you to connect with other reputable professionals on the site.

You earn RepScore points in the following three ways:

- **Community verification:** When you invite your contacts to join your network, you can ask some of them to act as references, giving you an endorsement to display in your profile. The more references, the more points you earn.

- **Profile completeness:** Earn RepScore points for completing all fields—or sections—of your Naymz profile and updating it periodically.

- **Identity verification:** Naymz has an alliance with Trufina (www.trufina.com), a personal information management service that verifies that you are who you say you are. You get the Trufina service free if you pay for the premium subscription to Naymz. You also earn RepScore points for doing so.

Step 3: Complete Your Profile

If you've joined LinkedIn or other social networks, and if you scripted a self-marketing sound bite in chapter 2, you probably have plenty of biographical and profile-type data on hand to use here. In the "About you" section, paste your bio, including past work history and educational credentials.

Under "Tags," list keywords you want associated with you—words that other people in the network or search engines could use to find you. These might be your areas of expertise, subject-matter knowledge, interests, functional roles, job titles, school names, employer names, hobbies, geographic location, and anything else that defines you.

You can also put links on your profile. These might be links to your blog or webfolio, your company Web site, other sites that relate to your field, or anything relevant to the image you want to project.

Step 4: Select the Service Level

Your final step is to decide whether you want to have the basic, free membership or upgrade to premium level for a low monthly fee (or pay for a year at a time to receive a discount). Among the perks that come with the premium membership are a sponsored link at or near the top of the page on Google, Yahoo!, and MSN search results for your name; an advertisement-free experience when people visit your profile; and a report on each person who visits your profile, including that person's city, state, country, and how he or she found you.

When you're up and running with Naymz, don't forget to visit Ziggs to see if you'd like to join its service as well.

Ziggs

Whereas the emphasis at Naymz is on identity management and reputation enhancement (with a hint of social networking thrown in for good measure), Ziggs touts itself as more of a total solution for managing not just your online brand, but also the groups of people in your world. A handy feature on Ziggs allows you to classify your contacts into categories such as work colleagues, family, charities, college friends, and more. This capability can make it easy for you to communicate or plan events with people who have various roles in your life.

Additional sites to consider beyond Naymz and Ziggs are Wink (www.wink.com), Spock (www.spock.com), and qAlias (www.qalias.com). Calling themselves "people search engines," Wink and Spock let you find people on the Web and also allow you to manage your own online presence by having a profile on their sites. Also offering an online profile, much like a webfolio, qAlias charges a modest monthly fee to host your online bio and other content about you that can help you be found more easily online.

Webfolios: Your 24/7 Resume

A webfolio is a Web site that serves as an online portfolio of you and your work. Webfolios are useful for job seekers as well as professionals who aren't actively looking for a new job but want to have a place to point people—sort of an online calling card.

Your webfolio can include your bio and resume, a summary of your career achievements, case studies demonstrating your experience and expertise, work samples, and more.

For an example of what is typically included in a simple but effective webfolio, see the screenshot of James Whiteley's site in figure 6.1. James had this site developed as a place to display his professional credentials, not necessarily for job seeking. He created the content for it with the help of an executive career coach, Deb Dib (www.executivepowerbrand.com), and worked with Mark Hovind (www.jobbait.com) to design and develop the site.

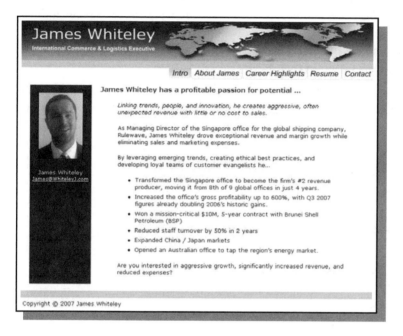

Figure 6.1: A sample webfolio for a professional not actively looking for a job.

Before You Start

Developing a basic Web site is surprisingly easy and inexpensive using templates provided by various hosting companies. Or you may opt to hire a professional Web designer, which often costs less than you might expect. Either way, you'll need to consider a few things before diving into the development of your site:

1. **Define your objectives for the site.** What do you want the site to do for you? Does it need to serve as an online resume to interest employers in hiring you? Or maybe you're not job seeking but want to establish your professional presence simply as a way to position yourself as a "player" in your organization or industry. Your webfolio can also be a handy reference tool for people who need to know

more about you when considering you for speaking engagements, board positions, volunteer roles, and more.

2. **Assemble your talking points.** In chapter 2 we guided you through the process of expressing who you are with a self-marketing sound bite that defines what you have to offer and what you're seeking (if anything). The content on your Web site needs to be concise and pack a punch, so keep your top strengths, unique attributes, and key value-added qualities in the forefront of your mind as you prepare to develop a webfolio that reflects you.

3. **Decide on a look and feel for your site.** Unlike a print resume or bio that is rather plain vanilla in terms of colors and graphics, your webfolio involves more aesthetic choices. The colors, layout, font style, and graphics on your site will reflect your image and your profession or career field. Browse other people's sites and think about what you want the look of your site to say about you.

Webfolio Hosting and Design Options

If you're serious about putting together a polished, impressive Web site to showcase your credentials and are not comfortable developing the site yourself, consider hiring a Web site designer. Professional Web designers charge either by the hour (typically ranging from teens per hour at the very low end to $50 or more per hour) or on a project basis, which could be in the hundreds or thousands of dollars.

> **Tip:** *Want to learn about good Web site design by viewing examples of bad design? Go to www. WebPagesThatSuck.com!*

Asking around for referrals to a designer is a good way to find one you can trust. It doesn't matter whether the designer is located in your city or town because you can communicate entirely by phone and e-mail. When choosing among designers, first review their own Web sites and samples of their work. Also speak with them by phone to get a feel for how easily you could work with them. Keep in mind that the designer you choose doesn't have to know your career field or industry; but he or she does need to have experience designing sites that are comparable in scope and style to how you want yours to turn out.

If you are reasonably comfortable with technology, we recommend considering the do-it-yourself options offered by hosting services such as Network

Solutions (www.networksolutions.com) and GoDaddy (www.godaddy.com), among others. The design and layout templates they offer are easy to use and produce clean, simple, and professional-looking sites for a modest price.

Writing Content for Your Webfolio

In its simplest form, a webfolio can be nothing more than a one-page site that has your name as the main header, your tag line (a simple statement conveying who you are or what you do) below the main header, and then your bio filling out the rest of the page. You might also include a photo, although this is optional.

A richer webfolio, yet still very easy to put together, contains about three to five pages. Most hosting services such as Network Solutions and GoDaddy offer a one-page or five-page Web site as the standard, with the option to pay extra for additional pages. An ideal three-page webfolio arrangement is described piece-by-piece in the following sections.

Page 1: Bio

The first (home) page gives your site's visitors an overview of your experience and credentials through a brief bio of a couple or few paragraphs. If you've prepared a profile for posting on social networking sites, you have content to use on this page.

Page 2: Career Highlights

Imagine yourself talking face-to-face with someone about the times in your professional life that you're the most proud of or that are the most interesting. If you wanted people to know three to five things about your career history, what would they be? They might be accomplishments and achievements, success stories from projects that turned out well, or case studies of problems you found solutions to or clients you did great work for. Anything along these lines provides good content for this page of your site.

Page 3: Resume

On the third page, you can provide your entire resume as a supplement to your bio. This is particularly important for anyone who is actively job seeking.

Creating Webfolio Content That Your Readers Will Read

- Write short sentences and short paragraphs.

- Make your most critical points early in a paragraph or section in case readers don't read all the way through. Start with the key idea and then fill in the details below it.

- Break up your text with subheadings rather than long blocks of text in paragraphs.

- Use lists, such as bullet-point lists, in place of some paragraphs.

- Use action-oriented language. Avoid passive verbs and dull wording.

- Proofread your content carefully and ask others to review it for you to spot any errors.

- Have plenty of white (blank) space around your text.

A Canadian study published in the journal *Behaviour and Information Technology* found that Web site readers form an opinion of a site in about one-twentieth of a second after only a quick scan of it, not a careful read. Keep this in mind as you develop your site. Less is more when it comes to Web content, as long as what you include has an impact.

Webfolios Versus Blogs

Blogs have just about burst the bubble of webfolios in that many experts such as career coaches and personal branding specialists now recommend blogs as a better way to showcase your expertise and connect with people in a more interactive manner. Blogs are more in keeping with recent Web trends (usually referred to as Web 2.0), which have made the Internet a more interactive place. Blogs provide a place to connect with others, start dialogs and conversations, and generally have a more dynamic experience than before.

We agree that blogs do have an edge over webfolios in many ways and are more in keeping with the times, but we also believe strongly in the value of webfolios as an online networking tool. Blogs take a great deal of time to maintain and typically aren't designed to include a lot of static content. Blogs usually do include the owner's bio, but the focus is more on the log of posts, comments, and archives of posts rather than on portfolio documents.

If blogging is not for you for any number of reasons, having a webfolio can be a relatively easy, low-maintenance way to have an online presence.

Discussion Groups

Online discussion groups have been around for years. Internet pioneers used these groups to find and keep in touch with individuals with similar interests. Although blogging has stolen much of the spotlight from discussion groups, these groups still play an important role in online networking. Let's look at the different types of discussion groups, how to join, and the advantages and disadvantages of joining.

> **Note:** *Remember that another alternative to having your own blog is commenting on other people's blogs. Doing so is one of the best ways to get your name out there and build your online brand.*

What Exactly Is a Discussion Group?

A discussion group is an online application that allows groups of people to share ideas, post messages, and hold discussions. Also known as Internet forums, bulletin boards, and message boards, these Web applications can be effective networking and marketing tools. Discussion groups encourage individuals with common interests to form online communities for sharing ideas, opinions, advice, and best practices in their fields.

Discussion groups first came into being as common-interest groups, whether personal or professional. They have more recently become popular with job seekers and people trying to network with professionals in their fields. People from around the world use these online groups to share knowledge, find inspiration, and search for career opportunities. When we say "professionals" from around the world, we truly mean it; you can easily find groups such as New Zealand Wellington Business Referral Club, Jobs-of-Egypt, Jobs in France, Seattle IT, Kansas Jobs, and All Bangalore Jobs. There is no limit to how far away from home, or close to home, these discussion groups can take you!

Why Use a Discussion Group and Not a Targeted E-mail List?

You could simply put together a list of e-mail addresses of likeminded people and communicate with each other via e-mail. So why communicate through a discussion group? Unlike e-mail lists, discussion groups allow you to archive messages, view shared photos, upload a group event calendar, and even post member profiles. They give all members a place to go, kind of like communal Web sites.

Group members have the option of checking the group Web site to read posted messages or receiving an e-mail alert whenever a new message or document is posted. Unlike with online chat rooms and instant messaging—in which communication is live, or concurrent—members of discussion groups do not have to be online at the same time to communicate with each other. You can post a question or comment at any time, and other members can sign into the group and post a reply at any time. And, unlike blogs, where only a select person (the author or owner) can post content and approve others' comments, discussion groups allow anybody to post items to share (but some do have moderators who approve comments before posting them).

Members often post their profiles in discussion groups. These are useful tools if you are trying to network for professional purposes. As a job seeker, you might be able to find a networking contact in your target company. Recruiters may spot potential candidates in discussion groups (assuming that they are searching in a professional/business-related discussion group).

You can also enhance your visibility in a discussion group. Being able to post and share documents is a great way to publicize an event that you are hosting or speaking at or an article that you have published. Discussion groups are a fast and free way to market yourself to thousands of people at any moment in time.

Where Can I Find Discussion Groups?

The most popular Web sites for discussion groups are Yahoo! and Google. These companies have made it easy (and free) to set up a discussion group within minutes. Don't have time to create your own unique group? Don't fret; thousands of existing groups are already out there on the Web. Locating them is just a matter of searching for the subject matter that interests you most.

Yahoo! boasts more than 35,000 discussion groups under its Employment & Work category. It has groups dedicated to certain companies (for example, McDonald's Employees), industries, associations, and small businesses.

Google has a total of more than 10,000 discussion groups, 60 of which are related to employment. As with Yahoo!, these discussion groups are easy to use and free to create. Google offers two types of discussion groups:

- **Traditional Usenet Google Groups:** The Usenet Google discussion groups are not hosted or moderated by one single organization. They are decentralized and unmoderated, meaning that anyone can post messages.

- **Non-Usenet Google Groups:** These are the more common discussion groups. They have one or more moderators or administrators (kind of like the owners of the group) who decide which messages can be posted to the group Web site. Moderators ensure that each post is appropriate to the group's original purpose. They can also choose who can subscribe to their group and whether nonmembers can view the group and post messages.

Google User Groups

Google has created some official groups to help you navigate its Web site and answer your questions. Refer to them if you ever get stuck or confused (not that we expect that to happen!). Some of the official Google Groups include

- Google Groups Guide
- Blogger Help Group
- Google Page Creator Discussion
- Google Webmaster Help

What Are the Benefits of Being a Group Member Versus Being a Moderator?

Being a moderator brings much more responsibility and time commitment. A moderator is often the same person who created the group in the first place. As a moderator, you are ultimately responsible for the content and activity of the discussion group. If you decide to create your own discussion group, be prepared to spend time each day (or every couple of days, depending on your schedule and the level of activity in the group) posting thought-provoking articles and other content on the group Web site. Remember, messages will be in an e-mail alert to each member, so make sure the content is relevant and interesting. Like having a blog, moderating a group means you need to draw in members by having an important discussion topic.

As a group member, on the other hand, you can be as passive or active as you choose, depending on your level of interest in the topics being discussed, your time availability, and how actively you need to be networking and getting exposure. If you are using discussion groups as part of your online identity, we suggest that you stay active. Certain people choose to join discussion groups and simply sit back, relax, and read what other members post. However, to get your name recognized as an important person in your profession, you need to be out there posting articles, suggesting Web sites, and publicizing relevant upcoming events. You want to be thought of as a mover and shaker in your field.

How to Start Your Own Group

Starting your own group is easier than you think and takes only a few minutes. First, decide whether you are going to use a Yahoo! or Google discussion group. Next, choose the theme/topic of your group. The sky's the limit: SAP applications, ways to relocate to a city with better jobs and climate, human resource professionals in Palm Springs— whatever you're interested in. Choose which category and subcategory your group will fit into. Remember, you want to make your group easy to find (so that you will have a lot of members), so put it in the category that makes the most sense.

> **Tip:** Don't be known as a "troll" or "gravedigger." These are individuals who post unwanted or derogatory messages. Be sensitive to the audience and post only messages that are of value. Nobody wants to read spam, cheesy sales advertisements, or your political opinions.

Choose a catchy group name and your group e-mail address, write a brief description of the group, and voila! You have created your own, unique discussion group. Following the simple directions provided by Google or Yahoo! to supplement what we've described here, you can begin posting messages and inviting new members immediately.

Electronic Publishing

The Internet has made it possible for everyone to get published. Whether through an article, a newsletter, or an entire book, anyone with a computer and something to say can be an author. Is this networking? Sure, it is. If networking is about gaining visibility to attract people and opportunities to you, as well as connecting with people to develop mutually beneficial relationships, online publishing fits the bill. The power of the pen—or, in this case, the keyboard—to connect with other human beings is often just as strong as connecting by voice or through a handshake.

Following are some electronic publishing options and tips for using them.

E-newsletters

One popular online publishing option is to publish some type of periodical. This can be in the form of a document you e-mail to a list of subscribers or content posted on a Web site. Your best option for publishing a periodical is to produce an electronic newsletter, which might come out weekly, bimonthly, monthly, or quarterly.

Just like a traditional print newsletter someone would receive in the mail, an e-newsletter usually includes a few or several short articles that are informational and/or editorial in nature, as well as perhaps some news and announcements of events that would interest your readers.

Numerous companies offer templates and distribution services for online newsletters. They charge a modest (often less than $20) monthly fee for the service. Constant Contact (www.constantcontact.com) is one of the best to use.

You can also go the do-it-yourself route and incur no cost. This simply means that you type a message in an e-mail and send it out to people, or create a document in PDF format and e-mail it as an attachment. The downside of this approach is that many people aren't going to want to open an attachment, either out of concern over computer viruses or because doing so is inconvenient. Sending your letter within the body of an e-mail (rather than as an attachment) is not necessarily a better option, though, because you don't know how the layout and format might become messed up in transmission. The publication that people receive may not have the professional, polished look you intended it to have.

If you're serious about wanting to communicate with your network through an electronic newsletter, using a service such as Constant Contact or one of the many others available is worth the cost.

E-zines

The earliest online periodic publication was the "e-zine," which was, and still is, a sort of online magazine. The first e-zines appeared in the 1980s as articles posted on the Bulletin Board System, or BBS—a precursor to the World Wide Web. In the 1990s, e-zines grew in popularity and were more likely to be distributed through e-mail via the Web. E-zines are a dying breed because blogging has taken over. They've become difficult to e-mail because of spam filters and don't offer the interactive qualities of blogs. Nevertheless, you might come across one from time to time or hear the term, so just be aware of what they are.

Articles, Wikis, and Lists

If you have your own Web site or blog, you certainly have plenty of opportunities to write and publish content, whether it's an article, editorial, or essay. You can educate, inform, provoke thought, amuse, and show off your knowledge and writing skill with online publishing.

Articles

You don't have to have your own site or blog to write articles. Many professional associations need content to keep their sites fresh and either actively solicit articles or accept unsolicited articles from both members and nonmembers. Just be sure your topic is relevant to the readership, contributes meaningful ideas and information, reflects your brand, and is well written.

Wikis

Wikis are Web site pages that anyone can edit. If you've ever gone onto a Web site and been frustrated by content that contains factual errors or could have been written more clearly, you'll like wikis. On a wiki, you can add to, delete, or modify what's been written, or introduce content on a topic that hasn't yet been written about on that site. Wikis are particularly useful for knowledge-sharing and are often collaborative, group efforts of academic, scientific, and technical professionals.

Lists

When we talk about lists in terms of the Internet, we can mean two different things. There is e-list technology, often called a "listserv," which is the software used to develop or manage electronic mailing lists. Then, there is "list" in the conventional sense of the word—a list of people, places, or things. In this case, though, it happens to be an electronic list.

The plain old list concept is what we're talking about here. People love lists. Been on Amazon.com lately? You can hardly pick out a book on a particular topic without bumping into a list of favorite books in that category that an ordinary reader has submitted to the site. In chapter 5, you learned that a list of favorite or recommended blogs, sometimes called a "blogroll," is typical sidebar content on a blog.

Lists created by regular people help us make choices about services or products to buy and events to attend. The person responsible for the list often becomes known as a thought leader in a particular field, and often as someone who helps his or her professional community.

In our metro area of Atlanta, Georgia, for example, The Ruthie List (www.ruthieslist.org) is a Yahoo! group with nearly 4,000 members who are recruiters and human resources professionals. The list is free and provides members with postings of open positions and available candidates and with updates on professional meetings and other happenings in the local HR and recruiting community. By offering this list for more than 10 years, senior HR professional Ruthie Powell has established herself not only as a leader in her professional community, but as someone who genuinely cares about helping that community.

Tip: *Don't feel you have to be a top-of-your-field, famous personality in your area of expertise to get a speaking gig. As long as you have a high degree of knowledge in a particular area, you'll do fine. You don't have to be an absolute expert who knows it all. Success in public speaking comes as much from having an engaging, energetic, and friendly but authoritative speaking style, as well as solid experience, as it does from your actual knowledge level. In other words, it's what you've done and how you talk about it that counts just about as much as what you know.*

Internet-Based Public Speaking

In chapter 3, we introduced you to the idea of public speaking as an element in your online networking repertoire. For some of you, that might have been the first time you thought of public speaking as networking. Others of you may have already experienced the value of speaking as a way to enhance your professional stature and expand your range of contacts but might not have taken your talents online.

With the broad reach that technologies such as podcasting and webinars offer, public speaking online can do wonders for your networking efforts.

Where to Find Speaking Opportunities

You can find public speaking opportunities online in much the same way you would offline opportunities. Professional and trade associations are among the most common sources. In the past, most associations have offered special talks to members primarily at national conferences and conventions or at the occasional local or regional meeting. But now many associations host ongoing series of Web-based lectures, training seminars, or other informational sessions because they are easier and cheaper.

If you're a member of an association, check to see whether there are any options for you to share your expertise and experiences with the membership. Or, if you're not an expert on a particular topic, you could possibly moderate a panel discussion or interview a guest speaker.

> **Tip:** *To find names and URLs of professional associations in various fields, use Yahoo's listings at http://dir.yahoo. com/business_and_ economy/organizations/ professional/ or Weddle's Association Directory at www.weddles.com/ associations/index.cfm. You can also find copies of the reference book* Gale's Encyclopedia of Associations *in many libraries. It's an excellent resource.*

Additional sources of online speaking opportunities are educational institutions (particularly distance-learning degree programs and training institutes that offer a lot of online programming), nonprofit organizations, corporations, speakers' bureaus, and individuals who work as meeting or event planning professionals.

How Podcasts Work

A podcast is a digital audio file that allows you to record a radio-style broadcast for distribution over the Internet for playback on MP3 players and personal computers. The term "podcast" can be both a noun referring to the content being broadcast or the actual event, as well as a verb, referring to the act of podcasting.

Podcasting has made it possible for anyone to become a radio talk show host of sorts. By having your own podcast, you can broadcast commentary about topics relevant to your profession or business arena, interview other experts in your field, or create any type of audio content that will help you present yourself as a thought leader in your field.

Similarly, by being a guest on someone else's podcast, you gain visibility and enhance your digital footprint. Podcasts are often archived on the sites where they originated, so over time people can listen to them repeatedly.

If you like the idea of having a blog to brand yourself as a spokesperson on particular topics and to start people talking, you'll probably love the idea of having your own podcast (unless you hate the sound of your speaking voice). Having a podcast is like being the host of a radio talk show. You can invite guests to interview or just talk to your audience, offering commentary and words of wisdom that position you as a leader in your field.

Starting a podcast is quite easy. It's not as easy as being the guest who just calls in (or is called) and answers some questions, however, because it does take time and planning. But the technology piece is fairly simple. With only a computer, a high-speed Internet connection, and an inexpensive microphone (probably the one that came with your computer will do fine), you can be on the air in a matter of hours.

You simply plan what you want to say (the niche focus of your program, not just today but for the long haul), record your first broadcast, create an MP3 file of the broadcast, and post it on the Internet. Okay, you need to know a few things about each of those steps, so this task is not quite as simple as we're making it sound, but it's pretty painless.

Where to Go for More Advice on Starting a Podcast

One of the best resources for developing a podcast is the advice provided by podcasting expert Jason Van Orden at his site www.how-to-podcast-tutorial.com. He offers easy-to-follow, free advice about getting started in podcasting. Although Jason does also sell products and services through his site, including a course on professional podcasting, we have been impressed by the truly useful, detailed advice offered on his site without bombarding readers with sales pitches for the money-making products.

How Webinars Work

Another option for getting your voice heard is to conduct or be a guest presenter in a webinar, which is essentially a seminar held on the Web or through a combination of Web and telephone. Webinars are typically held live, meaning that there is a start and end time, and your audience is listening to you while you're online and on the phone, rather than in a recorded session at a later time. Some webinars are recorded and archived on a Web site, however, for those who cannot attend the live event.

True webinars are entirely Internet-based. They use Web conferencing technology that employs Voice Over Internet Protocol (VoIP) for the presenters' voices to be conveyed computer to computer with no need for telephones. This audio component is complemented by a visual presentation online that typically resembles a PowerPoint slide presentation. Other webinars combine telephone conference calling for the audio portion with Web-based visual presentation.

Webinars are extremely convenient for both presenters and attendees. You can participate from anywhere that you have Internet access (with a working microphone and speakers if the audio portion is through VoIP) and/or a telephone. Another benefit of webinars is that they can be collaborative. Presenters can poll and survey the audience during the event, and attendees can ask questions, either by typing them online or speaking in a live chat.

> **Note:** *WebEx (www.webex.com), Microsoft's Live Meeting (http://office.microsoft.com/enus/livemeeting/default.aspx), and TelSpan (www.telspan.com) are three of your best bets for Web conferencing services.*

Whether through podcasting or webinars, you can make your presence known online and connect with many people, so we encourage you to consider speaking opportunities as part of your online networking strategy.

As you can see from the technologies surveyed in this chapter, there's something for everyone when it comes to networking online. Whether you prefer to write or speak, be the ringleader or just be in the peanut gallery, you'll find a place to connect with others and build your reputation online.

Key Points: Chapter 6

- Joining identity-management sites such as Naymz and Ziggs is a great way to control your online identity.

- A Webfolio is a Web site that serves as an online portfolio of you and your work. It can be used by job seekers to attract employers as well as by professionals who simply need a place to keep their credentials online.

- By joining discussion groups, you can gain visibility and forge relationships with likeminded professionals.

- Publishing e-newsletters, online articles, book reviews, and other online content is a great way to demonstrate and share your knowledge.

- Internet-based public speaking, including webinars and podcasts, establishes you as a thought leader in your field and can significantly expand the size of your network.

Chapter 7

Day Seven and Beyond: Keep It Going and Growing

Online networking is not a passing fad or flash-in-the-pan phenomenon. It's here to stay. All professionals need to make a commitment to online networking as a way of life and to using it as a vehicle to build mutually beneficial, long-term relationships and give back to others. This final chapter of the book provides action steps to help you put into practice what you've learned in the chapters leading up to this one, as well as valuable tips for enhancing and expanding your activities beyond the seven-day scope of this book.

In This Chapter

- Commit to taking action by developing an online networking plan.
- Get motivated by examples of how real people are using online networking in their careers and businesses.
- Take your online networking to the next level and make it last beyond Day Seven.
- Do's and Don'ts for proper online etiquette.
- Where online networking is heading in the future.

Develop Your Online Networking Action Plan

In the early chapters of this book, we helped you identify your career or business goals. After that, we laid out the virtual cafeteria of online networking activities in seven main categories—all the ways you could be spending your time.

Now, let's make the most of that valuable time by working on an action plan for your online networking efforts. As you now know, some methods require more effort than others. Some, such as a webfolio, require substantial start-up time but not much ongoing maintenance. Others, such as having your own blog, require frequent care and feeding. For an at-a-glance look at the pros and cons of each option in terms of time commitment required and benefits you'll reap, see the Online Networking Return On Investment (ROI) chart in figure 7.1.

	Initial Setup	Maintenance	Brand Expression	Writing Skill Needed	Low Tech	Cost	ROI
Social Networks	■		■		■	FREE or $-$$	A+
Profile Management Sites	■		■		■	FREE or $	B+
Blogs (your own)	■	■	■	■		$-$$	A
Blogs (others')			■	■	■	FREE	A+
Webfolios	■		■			$$-$$$	B–
Discussion groups (as a participant)			■	■	■	FREE	B
Online publishing	■		■	■		FREE	B+
Podcasts (your own)	■	■	■			FREE or $-$$	A–
Podcasts (others')			■				B+

LEGEND:
Initial Setup: Significant front-end investment of time needed
Maintenance: Significant, consistent, ongoing maintenance required
Brand Expression: Excellent way to communicate your brand (including ability to customize and personalize)
Writing Skill Needed: Must be able to communicate in written form clearly and concisely
Low Tech: No need for sophisticated knowledge of technology tools
Cost: FREE = no fee to participate; $ = low cost; $$ = moderate cost; $$$ = expensive
ROI: Your return on investment for your time, money, and effort

Figure 7.1: Online Networking Return On Investment (ROI).

There is no one-size-fits-all solution to online networking. The methods you use and time you choose to devote to it are based on a number of factors, including your needs and goals, time available, personal style, skills, and budget.

Your Needs and Goals

You might have an urgent need to land a job or to get a business off the ground and need to become as visible and connected as possible. Or maybe you just want to network for no particular reason other than to enhance your overall professional stature and stay in the know. There's no sense of urgency in that case, and you might be quite busy doing your "day" job, so you aren't planning to devote a lot of time to online networking.

Your Personal Style

Your personal style and skills play a role as well. Do you love to write, or can you barely put two sentences together? Blog writing doesn't require Pulitzer Prize–worthy journalistic talents, but you do need to have a reasonable amount of writing skill and the desire to do it. Are you on the introverted side and don't feel comfortable expressing yourself too openly for all the world to see? If so, you might be better suited to having a webfolio and a bio posted on a profile-management site rather than being fully "out there" expressing your opinions on your own blog or amassing thousands of contacts on LinkedIn.

Tip: Take out your appointment book or pull up your electronic calendar and make some dates with yourself. Schedule a recurring appointment on a daily, weekly, or at least monthly basis to devote to networking online. Otherwise, you might relegate this task to the proverbial backburner indefinitely.

These are only rough guidelines for what you should be doing. We encourage you to stretch beyond your comfort zone and not just take the easy way out. Introverts, for example, do need to put themselves out there sometimes and connect with others, not just network passively. Employed professionals do need to make an effort to carve out a few extra minutes and hours here and there for networking, whether or not they have an urgent need. Business owners shouldn't be so focused on drumming up new business to meet immediate revenue needs that they forget to cultivate longer-term referral sources. The examples could go on and on, but you get the picture. Network in a way that fits who you are, but also set some "stretch" goals to challenge yourself.

Four Speeds for Traveling the Online Roads

Let's get down to the business of planning exactly what steps you'll to take to start networking online or to boost your existing efforts. You have four basic options to choose from. Think of them as driving a car at four different speeds. You can creep down the driveway and not go anywhere else. You can amble down a country road at a moderate speed, stopping to smell the roses and take in the view at various spots. You can move swiftly down an expressway. Or you can put pedal to the metal and go even faster on the autobahn.

The Driveway

If you're new to online networking and want to start out slowly, or if you don't have any pressing short-term goals to work on and limited time to spend, you might want to go driveway speed. This can also be a good way to ease into the process if you're not real proficient with technology and prefer to take things slowly. Although there are many ways to approach the driveway option, we recommend taking the following steps:

1. Join LinkedIn or any professionally oriented social networking site relevant to your purposes. Develop a basic profile, invite a few friends and colleagues to join your network, and accept invitations that come your way.

2. Find two to three blogs that interest you (because they relate to your business or career field) and mark your calendar to read them once a week. You may even get up your nerve to comment on them.

3. Write a bio and post it on a profile-management site, such as Naymz or Ziggs.

4. Join a discussion group as an active reader instead of a participant.

At some point you will probably need to speed up the car and venture past the end of the driveway, but these four steps will help you start your journey.

The Country Road

Think about what a drive in the country is like. You're certainly going faster than in your driveway, but you're moving slowly enough to enjoy the scenery along the way. You might also decide to stop on the side of the road to take in a great view or fork off to the right instead of the left at an intersection just to see what's down that way. You might also make an unexpected stop at a roadside farm stand to pick apples and chat with the farmer. This is an apt analogy for surfing the Internet as a networker, because there are certainly plenty of places to stop and take in the view and lots of people to chat with.

With the country-road approach to online networking, you have a general destination in mind—your career or business goals. However, you're not in a big rush to get there, and you want to explore all the avenues to soak up information and meet new people. What does this approach look like in terms of action steps? It would include all the driveway steps plus the following:

1. Network more actively on LinkedIn or another social networking site of your choice. Use techniques covered in chapter 4 to develop a broader, larger network and to enhance your profile with endorsements and other bells and whistles.

2. Don't just lurk in the shadows of blogs, reading them without commenting. Find one or two sites most relevant to you that let you best express your personal brand and comment on them regularly. That might be once a week or could be more or less often. The point is to be consistent and involved.

3. Set aside some time each week (or each day if your schedule permits) to browse a variety of networking forums, including discussion groups and chat rooms; to join additional social network sites; to read or comment on more blogs; and to view the webfolios of people in your field.

> **Tip:** *No matter which of the four speeds you pick for your online networking journey, don't forget to Google yourself regularly to keep tabs on your online identity, as we recommended in chapter 2. You'll be leaving digital footprints all over the place, so you need to glance back at them occasionally to see what kind of trail you're leaving.*

The country-road method can be fun, but like an actual drive in the country, it isn't always fruitful. So just make sure that your efforts are focused enough to bring some results when you need them.

The Expressway

Have somewhere to go and need to get there as quickly as possible? The expressway is probably your best bet. This approach to online networking is focused and purposeful. Determine which networking methods are the most likely to help you reach your goals; then aim between the white lines and drive ahead until you get there.

This speed includes the driveway and country-road activities plus the following:

1. Create your own blog and keep it fresh with regular postings.

2. Develop a webfolio that showcases who you are and what you have to offer. Note that your blog typically would be a part of this Web site rather than a separate location so that you can drive traffic to just one place.

3. More actively manage your membership in LinkedIn or other social networks. This step might include posting and answering questions in the experts' section, digging even deeper for people to invite to join your network, and paying the premium fee for increased access to the membership at-large.

4. Pay the premium fee for an upgraded membership in profile-management sites such as Ziggs and Naymz so that you get more visibility for your profile and better placement in search engines.

The expressway route is most likely for you if you're actively job searching or looking to develop business or significantly enhance your professional stature.

The Autobahn

Ever traveled on the actual autobahn in Germany or the high-speed motorways of some other countries? Then you know that rarely do cars on those roads travel the recommended 130 kilometers per hour (about 80 miles per hour). The speeds are usually much faster than that, or at least they seem that way when the cars fly up behind you with lights flashing. Well, you might choose to travel that fast in your online networking to meet your objectives.

The autobahn route includes all activities from the lower speeds plus some advanced techniques to skyrocket your visibility and connectivity. Not for the faint of heart, this approach to online networking is for those who can commit serious time and energy to it. In addition to blogging and maintaining an up-to-date Web site about yourself or your business, you will add strategic, subject-matter-expert contacts to your network; get published online as often as possible; host a podcast; or seek interview opportunities on others' podcasts. You'll publish a regular e-newsletter and maybe host a discussion group or maintain an e-list.

If you are looking to land a job as quickly as possible or heavily promote yourself as an entrepreneur, the autobahn might be the online networking route for you. Just be sure not to confuse quantity with quality; you would be better off doing fewer things but getting it right than spreading yourself too thin and having the quality suffer.

How Real People Are Networking Online

You may already be on your way toward your online networking goals. Or you might still be at the starting point, unsure which options to pick to drive your online networking strategies. We certainly hope that by now you're not skeptical about the value of online networking!

Whichever your situation, we want to help you become or stay motivated by sharing some of the many comments we've heard from online networkers. These comments came to us from online networkers in every region of the United States and on three other continents. They're from our own clients and colleagues as well as fellow social networking members (primarily LinkedIn) who have responded to questions we've posted to survey members about their experiences.

Comments About Social Networking Sites

- An IT consultant in Europe is on Plaxo, LinkedIn, Ecademy, XING, and Ryze. Primary platform (most effective) is XING.

- A human resources professional located in the Midwest likes LinkedIn for doing people research by company and industry.

- A technology executive in the Southeast likes Plaxo because it works easily with LinkedIn. He is also a member of Ecademy but finds that site less helpful because it has fewer U.S. members. He also has a profile on Naymz.

- In Brazil, a young professional has had two job offers as a result of LinkedIn recruiter contacts. She also likes Plaxo because of the open access to contact information. She previously tried a locally focused networking site but found it less effective.

- An Atlanta engineer, in job search due to a layoff, received a LinkedIn invitation from a former coworker, now at another company. He accepted the invitation and was then invited to apply for a position at the new company. He believes his former coworker was sending strategic LinkedIn invitations to fill an open position. Fill it he did, with this engineer, and within a week of initial contact.

- A supply-chain consultant rates LinkedIn as the most professional of all the social networking sites but doesn't like some of the rules that discourage open networking. He likes Plaxo's unlimited invitations policy and believes it will soon be a strong competitor for LinkedIn. He has tried other global sites but found them way behind LinkedIn and Plaxo in membership and features.

- New to Plaxo, an Atlanta HR specialist accepted a couple of invitations and "suddenly things seem to be connecting everywhere." She's concerned about trying to keep current on both sites and worried that duplication of effort could detract from her job search time. She likes LinkedIn both for job search and for reconnecting with old friends.

- Preferring Plaxo for contact management, a business owner isn't sure yet how effective it will be as a networking platform. He has made contacts on LinkedIn that have taken business relationships to a new level. If he were to use just one tool, it would be LinkedIn.

- A senior finance executive moved to a new location where she had no network. She was sourced on LinkedIn by four recruiters, contacts that ultimately yielded two offers. Her advice to others: "Post a complete profile, always respond promptly to calls, make yourself available quickly for interviews, and refer others if the opportunities aren't a fit for you. Above all, remember the networking tool only opens the door. Then it's up to you!"

- A mid-career HR generalist appreciated our willingness to accept her invitation to connect on LinkedIn. She has found that not too many people are receptive to blind invites because they don't know the individual. Her theory is that this is how you get to know people and expand your existing network.

- A sales professional used LinkedIn to review the profiles of company managers he was scheduled to meet for interviews. He believes that advance information made the difference in one interview, and he is still working at the organization today.

- A job seeker finds that company interviewers are comparing data in his social networking profiles to the information in his resume. He's not sure if recruiters are using social networking sites but knows that prospective employers are doing so.

Recruiters React to LinkedIn and Other Sites

- A U.S.–based recruiter and regular LinkedIn user has recently added Viadeo to his networking regimen, although he expects its strong European focus to be less useful for his primarily U.S.–based search practice.

- LinkedIn has been a great business development, sourcing, and job searching tool for a technology recruiter. He has experienced success in all three areas.

- A recruiter located in India shared that LinkedIn has affected her recruiting business "tremendously." She describes it as a very powerful professional networking tool, one of the few with a widespread awareness the world over.

- A recruiter in the northeastern United States benefits from LinkedIn as a passive recruiting tool (people find and approach him), as a candidate sourcing tool, and as a way to sketch out an org chart for a target company (when you have a large enough network).

- A recruiter with a large network on LinkedIn acknowledges that he's found some good candidates and has penetrated larger accounts via LinkedIn. But "in the end, it doesn't hold a candle to picking up the phone and working it the old fashioned way."

Bloggers Speak Out on Blogging

These comments are responses to a question we posed on LinkedIn: "Do you blog for business or personal reasons?" Fewer than 20 percent of the respondents described their blogs as purely personal. Many answered "both," citing both personal and professional benefits.

- Pushing herself to make frequent posts, a technology professional finds doing that forces her to keep up-to-date on her field and enables her to share that knowledge with fellow professionals.

- An IT manager regards blogs as very important for online business. He finds that keywords in blogs are ranked highly by search engines.

- A statistician in Europe is using her blog to help with her job search.

- A career consultant blogs to make up-to-date information available to clients. He also encourages his clients to increase their Internet presence through blogs and other media.

- A professional writer blogs for personal reasons. In her work, she is usually writing in another person's or organization's voice on topics that may or may not reflect her personal interests. Blogging provides a vehicle for her to write in her own style and voice on a subject she's passionate about.

- An executive coach has three blogs and posts to each on a daily basis, which increases hits on his Web site. He calls them "One of the most effective marketing techniques available!"

- A marketing communications manager blogs for personal reasons but acknowledges that blogging has expanded both personal and professional networks.

- Choosing to blog on a niche professional topic that was not being adequately covered, a programmer blogs for multiple reasons: to help organize his thinking on the subject, to elicit comments from others, and to serve as a resource for others.

- An author and entrepreneur started blogging in support of a book she wrote. Today she blogs for her own company and is a blog consultant to other businesses.

- Blogging for professional reasons, a college counselor derives personal satisfaction from the process.

- A business executive started blogging to fill an information gap in his area of specialty. But he cautions that "no one should blog unless they are passionate about their subject and have something sensible to say."

- Stimulated to blog for both personal and business reasons, an engineer currently in job search mode is careful about content that will show up in a Web search. He has also previously contributed to a corporate blog.

- An entrepreneur is homebound due to illness. Blogging and the use of social networking is "becoming my virtual mouth to speak about my opinions, thoughts, dreams (both personal and business)."

We've enjoyed hearing these opinions and learning from the experiences of online networkers around the globe. Although they work in many different fields and their online networking goals and activities are widely divergent, you can see the common themes that emerge. We hope these comments spark ideas in you and encourage you to take action with your own online networking efforts.

Beyond Day Seven

The scope of this book is designed to get you to Day Seven, equipped with lots of knowledge about online networking and a preliminary action plan to help you start. We don't want to leave you hanging there, though, so we now offer some tips for what you can do beyond the seventh day.

After you travel on your online journey for a while, you should feel confident and comfortable with your initial strategies and techniques and start to reap benefits from the process. You'll probably also be ready to take your networking activities to greater heights, so we've put together some advanced tips for you.

Bump Up Your Blog or Webfolio a Notch

- Develop a marketing plan for your blog or webfolio. You want to grow your readership and get maximum benefit from your investment of time.

- Add audio and video to your blog or Web site. Studies show that blogs with audio and video have a larger readership.

- Pay attention to search engine optimization for your blog or site. Add keywords and tags to increase your hits. Technorati is a good source for popular tags. Make sure your entry titles contain the right keywords to drive traffic to your blog.

- Add a "Digg This" button to your blog so that readers who "dig" your post can submit it to Digg, a news site that rates news stories and posts.

- Interview others for your blog, invite other writers to contribute posts, and be a guest blogger on other sites.

- Link all your social networking profiles to your blog or webfolio and include your blog URL, webfolio URL, and/or LinkedIn URL in your e-mail signature. Link to your own entries to encourage readers to spend a longer time on your blog.

- Learn to use feeds. They make it easy for people to read your blog and help you follow a network of blogs.

- Use blogging software with post-dating options to allow you to schedule advance dates for posting new content to your blog.

- Build connections with blog authors. Write directly to an author to show your interest in a particular post or general blog content. When you give attribution to a blog writer, provide a link directly to that blog post.

- Build connections with your blog readers. Include your e-mail address on your blog. Inviting e-mail communication (as opposed to relying strictly on communicating via comments) will encourage interaction and build relationships.

- Notify your network when you have made significant changes to your webfolio.

- Continue to evolve as a thought leader in your field. If your blog shows you to be a thought leader in your industry, it's also known as a "thlog."

Work the Social Networks Harder

- Explore and experiment when choosing your online networking platforms. Try a number of online discussion groups, check out multiple blogs in your areas of interest, and join several social networking sites. After a while, if a site isn't working for you, find a more productive alternative. Be active on the sites that you ultimately select.

- Be aware that employers and recruiters may use LinkedIn to conduct informal "behind-the-scenes" reference checks. They can search for individuals who worked with you at your previous places of employment, not necessarily people that you included on your reference list. Make sure that recruiters and prospective employers know if you are conducting a confidential job search.

- By the same token, use LinkedIn to check out a prospective employer. In the search window, uncheck "Current Company" to find people who have left the organization (possibly a more objective viewpoint).

- Use LinkedIn to research your interviewers in advance of the interview and to get to know your new colleagues after you land a new role.

- Learn to use Boolean logic to create more precise search criteria. For example, use (**HR OR "human resource" OR "human resources"**) to identify contacts with any of those variations in their titles.

- Make sure you are alerted promptly to inmails, introductions, invitations, questions, and network updates. In "Accounts and Settings" … "Receiving Messages," elect to receive individual e-mails immediately.

- Gain visibility on LinkedIn by answering questions posed to the network. Post your own questions.

- Secure endorsements. Have a balanced number for each role.

- Periodically export your LinkedIn contacts and import them into a contact management application for tracking there.

- Consider upgrading your membership in LinkedIn to be able to send more introductions and inmails, and have access to more of the network.

- Notify your network when you have made significant changes to your social networking profiles. You can adjust your account settings to do this automatically.

- To avoid the risk of LinkedIn shutting down your account should five people decline to join your network, approach people initially via e-mail about connecting with you. After they agree to connect, you can invite them through LinkedIn.

- Connect to "power networkers," also known as "hubs." These are people with large networks on LinkedIn. Linking to them can help you build your network quickly. Many of the LinkedIn user groups list members with large networks.

- Join groups on LinkedIn. Depending on how groups are structured, they might give you easier access to LinkedIn members who are not part of your network but are part of the group. You can find groups through the site map at the bottom of every LinkedIn page.

- Join only as many social networking sites as you can comfortably manage.

- Grow your network strategically. Make sure you are adding key contacts, not just more contacts.

- Invite people you meet at offline networking events to join your LinkedIn network. It's a great follow-up after a networking event.

Do's and Don'ts for Proper Netiquette

In each of the preceding chapters, we've provided tips, including do's and don'ts, for each specific type of online networking. Here now are some key overall points and practices to help you get the most and give the best in all your online networking activities. They will help you behave like a solid "netizen":

1. Look and listen before you leap. On all online networking platforms, spend some time observing the tone, content, and contributors before joining the discussion. First impressions are lasting ones! Make sure that the first impression others have of you is favorable.

2. Help other people achieve their networking goals. Willingly facilitate introductions and consistently suggest resources and people who might be helpful to your contacts.

3. Don't spam your network contacts. Being pushy and self-serving will damage your online reputation, and the damage may be irreparable.

4. Keep your word. Follow through on any actions you promise to take. And do so in a timely manner.

5. Show appreciation when others provide assistance to you and to your contacts. Saying thank you is always appropriate and will encourage that person to provide assistance to you and others again.

6. Don't overwhelm your contacts with too many requests for introductions and assistance. Be considerate of their time and never give their e-mail addresses to others without permission.

7. Be respectful, courteous, and honest in all your online networking activities. Be positive and professional. Don't say anything that you wouldn't want aired on national news or shared with your mother!

8. Keep in mind that you are communicating with a global audience and that your language usage and cultural references might need to be understood by a very diverse set of people.

9. Allow time for networking. Make networking a part of your plan. Remember that networking provides some of the best opportunities to learn, grow, and give back. It's the number-one source for new jobs and new clients. So focus on becoming a skilled networker and budget time in your schedule for both online and offline networking activities.

10. Give and take. Networking is always about building relationships, not just seeking favors. It must ultimately benefit both parties. If you think only about what you need and want from the interaction, you will miss many opportunities to share experiences and enrich your life.

The Future of Online Networking

Benjamin Franklin is credited with saying: "In this world, nothing is certain but death and taxes." In the world of online networking, nothing is certain but growth and change! Making specific long-range predictions is difficult because the landscape is changing so much and so quickly. But the following statements describe the current state of affairs:

- More sophisticated technologies are yielding increased development options, site and software features, and networking benefits.

- The number of blogs continues to grow at a phenomenal rate.

- More social networking sites are starting every day, many catering to niche markets, including the baby boomer and "gray" demographics.

- Social networking sites will increasingly partner with other companies that offer technology to complement their own offerings. These partnerships are called "mashups" and should lead to enhanced user benefits.

- The number of people on social networking sites is growing by the millions every month, with the major sites still getting most of the traffic.

- More senior-level managers are becoming involved with online networking as a way to demonstrate thought leadership, showcase experience, and market themselves.

- More recruiters and companies are using search engines to find and qualify candidates. All professionals therefore need to have a significant and positive Internet presence or risk being screened out or viewed as not up-to-date on technology.

- More businesses are starting blogs to communicate with employees, customers, and shareholders.

- Major corporations are looking for social networking acquisitions and vying for position. Google owns Orkut. Rupert Murdoch bought MySpace and as of this writing was talking with LinkedIn.

Online networking is evolving but clearly here to stay. It's an exciting time for online networking...certainly more exciting than death and taxes! (Be sure to check our site, www.7days2onlinenetworking.com, for updates on how online networking is evolving.)

But, in the midst of this frenetic growth and change, we need to remind ourselves that it's still about networking and connecting with people. Vincent Wright, recruiter and power networker, summed it up for all of us by saying:

> These are times of important technological change. The reach and the possibilities are extraordinary.... It's now easier than ever to reach hundreds, thousands, millions of people. [Yet] there is one...little thing that we have to continue to master...how to be social to one another...how to work towards building friendships.... It's NOT about the technologies. It's about human relationships.

We count all of you as our new friends and colleagues and send you our very best wishes for online networking successes and rich and varied human relationships!

Key Points: Chapter 7

- To ensure that you put into practice what you've learned about online networking, develop a plan that takes into account your needs, goals, personal style, and level of urgency around reaching your goals.

- The authors' survey of actual people using social networking sites and blogs revealed a wide range of uses and success stories that might give you ideas for your own networking strategy.

- When you feel comfortable with the basics of online networking, tackle some more advanced steps to enhance your social networking, blogging, and other networking methods.

- The common thread in online networking etiquette is to be respectful and considerate of others and make networking a two-way street that benefits not just you, but also those in your network.

- Predicting the future of online networking is difficult because the landscape is changing so rapidly. But the one certainty is that online networking technologies will be an important part of any career management or business development effort for a long time to come.

Appendix

Recommended Resources

The resources listed here are intended to guide you further in your online networking efforts. Some resources have already been mentioned elsewhere in this book but are listed here in one handy place for your convenience. Other resources are new to the appendix. We've made every effort to list up-to-date resources with staying power, but in this rapidly changing world of online networking, it is always possible that some sites may be defunct, books out of print, or people out of business by the time you read this list.

These resources are organized into the following categories:

- Assessments
- Blogging
- Books
- Career Advice
- Discussion Groups
- Domain Names and Web Site Hosting
- Personal Branding and Identity Management
- Professional Association Directories
- Public Speaking, Publishing, and Podcasting
- Search Engines
- Social Networks

Assessments

The Web sites listed here offer assessment exercises and tests, or direct you to other sites that offer them. These assessment tools can help you identify your strengths and other unique attributes that define your personal brand, as discussed in chapter 2.

Riley Guide

www.rileyguide.com

This comprehensive Web site is a good starting point for finding assessment tools. Assessments listed or linked to include interest inventories, personality type indicators, skills assessments, and values inventories. Some assessments listed are self-directed, including some that are free, whereas others require an expert to administer and/or interpret the results, usually for a fee.

Brief Strengths Test and VIA Signature Strengths Questionnaire

www.authentichappiness.sas.upenn.edu

Dr. Martin Seligman is an acclaimed psychologist and founder of positive psychology, a branch of psychology that focuses on the empirical study of positive emotions, strengths-based character, and healthy institutions. His research has been published in *American Psychologist*, the journal of the American Psychology Association.

The Authentic Happiness site has almost 700,000 registered users and includes a self-directed testing center. The Brief Strengths Test and VIA Signature Strengths Questionnaire are excellent instruments for taking stock of your distinctive characteristics. All resources on the site are free; however, your responses to any of the assessment exercises may be used anonymously by researchers in the Positive Psychology Center of the University of Pennsylvania.

The Keirsey Temperament Sorter

www.keirsey.com

The Keirsey Temperament Sorter is a well-known assessment tool designed by David Keirsey, Ph.D., to help individuals discover their personality type and gain insight into themselves. The Keirsey test has been used by more than 35 million individuals since it was first published in 1978. You can take the Keirsey online and get a brief report free, or pay about $20 or less for more in-depth reports. The site also offers free membership in the Personality Zone, where you'll find advice, customized content for your type, and opportunities for social networking.

The Myers-Briggs Type Indicator

www.mbticomplete.com

The Myers-Briggs Type Indicator is another personality measure that has been taken by millions of people and has been around for decades. This very popular, well-respected tool is usually administered and interpreted by a certified MBTI practitioner. You can, however, take a self-directed, online version of the Myers-Briggs test on the MBTI Complete site for a fee of about $60.

The Self-Directed Search

www.self-directed-search.com

The Self-Directed Search (SDS) is an easy and quick but powerful assessment tool based on the Holland Code, a system developed by psychologist Dr. John L. Holland to assist people with finding careers that are best suited to their interests and abilities. You can take the SDS online and receive your personalized results report onscreen for about $10.

Blogging

Check out the following sites for more information on blogs and blogging:

Blogger: www.blogger.com

Drupal: http://drupal.org

Movable Type: www.sixapart.com

Technorati: www.technorati.com

TypePad: www.typepad.com

Vox: www.vox.com

WordPress: www.wordpress.com

Books

Blog Schmog, Robert Bly, Nelson Books, 2006

Blogging for Business, Shel Holtz and Ted Demopoulos, Kaplan Business, 2006

Blogging for Dummies, Brad Hill, Wiley Publishing, 2006

Career Distinction, William Arruda and Kirsten Dixson, Wiley Publishing, 2007

The Complete Idiot's Guide to Creating a Web Page & Blog, Paul McFedries, Penguin Group, 2004

I'm On LinkedIn—Now What??? Jason Alba, HappyAbout, 2007

The LinkedIn Personal Trainer, Steven Tylock, Tylock & Company, 2007

Networking for Job Search and Career Success, Michelle Tullier, JIST Publishing, 2004

The Unofficial Guide to Landing a Job, Michelle Tullier, Wiley Publishing, 2005

The Virtual Handshake, David Teten and Scott Allen, AMACOM, 2005

Career Advice

The following professional organizations include members who offer career counseling or coaching services to individuals to help with networking strategy, job search, and career management:

Career Counselors Consortium: www.careercc.org

Career Management Alliance: www.careermanagementalliance.com

National Career Development Association: www.ncda.org

Discussion Groups

Discussion groups are great places to meet like-minded people and share your opinions.

Google: http://groups.google.com

Yahoo!: http://groups.yahoo.com

Domain Names and Web Site Hosting

The following sites can help you get your own Web site or webfolio up and running:

DreamHost: www.dreamhost.com

GoDaddy: www.godaddy.com

Network Solutions: www.networksolutions.com

pairNIC: www.pairnic.com

Register.com: www.register.com

Personal Branding and Identity Management

The following sites will help you establish or manage your online identity and develop your personal brand:

Naymz: www.naymz.com

qAlias: www.qalias.com

Reach Branding Club: www.reachbrandingclub.com

ReputationDefender: www.reputationdefender.com

Spock: www.spock.com

Squidoo: www.squidoo.com

Wink: www.wink.com

Ziggs: www.ziggs.com

Professional Association Directories

To find names and URLs of professional associations in various fields, check out the following:

Yahoo!: http://dir.yahoo.com/business_and_economy/ organizations/professional

Weddle's Association Directory: http://www.weddles.com/ associations/index.cfm

Gale's Encyclopedia of Associations: A reference book available in many libraries

Public Speaking, Publishing, and Podcasting

These sites will help you get your written message published and your spoken words broadcast to enhance your online visibility.

Amazon book reviews: www.amazon.com

Constant Contact: www.constantcontact.com

How to Podcast: www.how-to-podcast-tutorial.com

Microsoft's Live Meeting: http://office.microsoft.com/en-us/ livemeeting/default.aspx

TelSpan: www.telspan.com

WebEx: www.webex.com

Wikipedia: www.wikipedia.org

Search Engines

The following are excellent portals for searching the Web:

About: www.about.com

AlltheWeb: www.alltheweb.com

AltaVista: www.altavista.com

Ask: www.ask.com

ChaCha: www.chacha.com

Dogpile: www.dogpile.com

GigaBlast: www.gigablast.com

Google: www.google.com

Google Alert: www.google.com/alerts

MSN: www.msn.com

SearchEngineWatch.com: www.searchenginewatch.com

Yahoo!: www.yahoo.com

Social Networks

Use one or more of the following social networking sites to post your profile and develop mutually beneficial professional relationships:

Amodus: www.amodus.org.uk

Blue Chip Expert: www.bluechipexpert.com

Bright Circles: www.brightcircles.com

Ecademy: www.ecademy.com

ExecuNet: www.execunet.com

Facebook: www.facebook.com

Go Big Network: www.gobignetwork.com

Hoovers Connect: www.hooversconnect.com

Konnects: www.konnects.com

LinkedIn: www.linkedin.com

The LinkedIn Blog: http://blog.linkedin.com/ (the corporate blog of the social networking site LinkedIn)

MyLink500 Top LinkedIn Members: http://mylink500.com

Mashable: www.mashable.com (a blog about social networks)

Network 2 Connect: www.network2connect.com

Networking for Professionals: www.networkingforprofessionals.com

Plaxo: www.plaxo.com

Ryze: www.ryze.com

Spock: www.spock.com

Spoke: www.spoke.com

Viadeo: www.viadeo.com

Wink: www.wink.com

XING: www.xing.com

Zubka: www.zubka.com

Index

X–Z

Notes

Notes

Notes

Notes

Notes